Policeman's Prelude

Harry Cole was born and brought up in Bermondsey, south London. He left school when he was fourteen, during the war, and became a cricket-bat maker, soldier, stonemason and, in 1952, a policeman. For thirty years, until his retirement in 1983, he served at the same police station in London.

He is a qualified FA coach (he has run numerous junior football teams), a referee and a keen cricketer. For many years he had a regular column in the *Warren*, the police magazine. His other books are *Policeman's Progress*, *Policeman's Lot*, *Policeman's Patch*, *Policeman's Patrol* and *Policeman's Story*, the second volume of his autobiography, of which this is the first, *Policeman's Gazette* and *The Blue Apprentices*, a novel.

In 1978 Harry Cole was awarded the British Empire Medal for voluntary work. Since leaving the force, in addition to writing he has taken up after-dinner speaking.

Harry Cole

Policeman's Prelude

FONTANA/Collins

First published in Great Britain
in 1982 by Fontana Paperbacks,
8 Grafton Street, London W1X 3LA
Fourth impression June 1988

Copyright © Harry Cole 1982

Printed and bound in Great Britain by
William Collins Sons & Co. Ltd, Glasgow

To Joan,
for putting up with
me and Max Miller

Contents

1. Collinson Street

The rearing black stallions faced each other eye to eye, their forelegs sparring like two nervous fighters afraid to strike the first blow. The flared nostrils and wide staring eyes conveyed all the fine balance between frightened anger and blind terror. With the artificial light reflecting clearly against those superb flanks, each of them balanced wonderfully still on hind hooves. The immobility of their pose served one invaluable purpose – it prevented the large, round clock that rested between them from rolling off the kitchen mantelpiece.

Within one minute, that monstrous old family timepiece would grandly announce the hour to the impatient six-year-old who sat staring up at its yellowing cracked face. From deep inside the bowels of its mechanism, grindings and whirrings would gather momentum. Cogs and springs would take up the noise and all would mysteriously blend into deep resonant chimes that vibrated all over the house.

Five . . . six . . . seven! At last, seven o'clock!

Everything happened in our house at seven o'clock. Mum would return home from her evening office cleaning job; I could have my supper; and granddad would go to the lavatory and count his money. This secret accountancy was not as pointless as it might first appear. The small terraced house that was 1 Collinson Street, Southwark, housed three families, and privacy was at a premium. Where better to sit and count one's loose change than in the backyard lavatory?

Granddad's secrecy was marred by the fact that he could only count aloud: 'Five shillings and tenpence ha'penny, five shillings and elevenpence ha'penny . . .' So many times I had seen my cloth-capped and pinafored grandmother listening intently at the flaking wooden door to ascertain whether the old man was as financially insolvent as he always claimed to be. 'Why, that wicked old sod,' she would cry to no-one in particular. 'He told me he was skint!' In retrospect, I doubt if she was ever as surprised as she seemed. Granddad made a point of telling everyone that he was skint.

The nightly arrival of granddad at the privy was no mundane, run-of-the-mill happening. On the contrary, there was a well-drilled, long-established ceremony that had to be performed come rain or shine, summer or winter. It was all a part of the nightly seven o'clock ritual.

Around the time that the clock made its first whirrings, granddad's slow, deliberate footsteps could be heard descending the bare wooden stairs. His route would take him along a short passageway and into our kitchen. We – mum, dad, my soon-expected brother and me – lived on the ground floor. My grandparents, together with a couple of mum's brothers and sisters, lived on the first floor. The Nash family, seven in number, lived at the top. With just three bedrooms in the whole house there were few secrets.

It would be fair to assume that most people divest themselves of at least some clothes in order to go to the lavatory. Granddad was different – he put them on. His jacket, his boots and his black felt cap. The peak of this sartorial elegance was reached with his white silk scarf. Granddad rarely wore a collar or a tie; he felt that with such a splendid silk scarf such items were dispensable. He made just a token gesture to formality by his use of a brass collar-stud. This he sported like a jewel in the turban of an eastern potentate.

Granddad would pass through our kitchen on his way to the outside toilet. As he reached the yard door he would pause and tuck in his scarf, each day – same place, same time. Thus attired, he would complete his journey out into the yard and the ultimate sanctuary of the lavatory. There, for a few precious minutes, he would be safe from all prying eyes, but not, of course, ears.

There were two other members of the Cole household: Tim, our belligerent cat, and Pie-Shop, our schizophrenic dog. Tim had been acquired for the sole purpose of catching some of the mice that scuttled cheerfully around the house. I can honestly say that he had not been one of my father's better purchases. Tim attacked just about everything *except* mice. His specialities were pigeons and old ladies.

Pigeons he would catch by the dozen. He would then crawl furtively into the house and deposit them, usually in the deep dark cupboard under the stairs. Sometimes, by way of variation and depending on his mood, he would slide them under the chest of drawers that stood behind the door in the bedroom. I think on reflection he enjoyed that most. The effect on my mother was certainly more dramatic. He would watch with mild interest from a safe distance. Then, as the first of her screams were emitted, he would saunter with a satisfied air in the direction of the backyard.

Although in general he appeared to be a fairly consistent cat – he hated just about everyone – I think he possibly hated women a little more than he hated men. The reason I say this is because of his favourite trick. The happiness on his face as he performed it was really quite moving. Tim

11

would curl up on our ground-floor windowsill and bask contentedly in the sun. He was a most impressive-looking animal: very big, with a stunning bright white and jet-black coat. Passers-by, particularly elderly ladies who did not know his reputation, would pause in admiration. This was their first mistake. Then they would offer a few words, usually along the lines of, 'Who's a lovely pussy then?'

The natural follow-up to this was to stroke their hands along his beautiful fluffy coat. Tim would purr sensuously and slowly close his eyes as if lost in some mysterious feline pleasure. The admirer would usually chortle at this stage: 'Yes, you like that, then, don't you?' It was at this moment that Tim would casually drag the claws from both front paws smoothly across the back of his masseuse's hand. There was, on average, a second's pause before the blood gushed. I used to find this interval quite fascinating. People can change their moods so very quickly.

Pie-Shop, on the other hand, was at peace with the world, although he would from time to time wake from a deep slumber and run frantically around the room. These sprints, lasting around five minutes, would scatter mum's proud collection of small carpets and rugs to all four corners. He would then return to his basket under the kitchen sink and fall instantly asleep. There were no half measures with Pie-Shop; he was either running flat out or not moving at all. Pie-Shop and Tim shared a complete lack of interest in each other. Thus harmony was maintained.

Strictly speaking, George and Rebecca, our two goldfish, should rate a mention, yet somehow they never seemed to count. If Tim was having a particularly frustrating day with his pigeons, he might spend a little time trying to paw them out of their bowl but even this excitement soon palled. Basically these two fish were extremely boring, yet they were also astonishingly resilient. On three separate occasions they were found on the floor. They could also go for days without a crumb of food, then guiltily I would inundate them with ants' eggs.

Their ending, however, was extremely dramatic. Space being at a premium, they were usually kept on the kitchen windowsill. One morning, after a particularly cold night, I discovered that the water, together with George and Rebecca, had frozen solid. This presented me with a problem. I quite believed that those two fish were capable of surviving any catastrophe, yet I also felt that in this situation I could use a little advice. But dad had gone off to the factory and mum was scrubbing offices. In those circumstances, what steps does a six-year-old take when his fish are frozen solid? My grandmother, whose unenviable task it was to feed me and prepare me for school, was, after all, a very elderly lady. (She must have been all of fifty!) No old lady could reasonably be expected to solve a problem as intricate as two frozen fish. All I had to do was to give the problem some thought. The ice had imprisoned the fish? Very well, if I thawed the ice then the fish would be free. Simple. But how?

Of course! The gas-stove! I had never been permitted to use the stove, in fact I was strictly forbidden to go anywhere near it, but I had seen my parents use it and it looked easy enough, and anyway this was an emergency. All I had to do was place the bowl on the gas-ring and light the gas. You surely didn't have to be grown up to do anything as simple as that?

Reassuring George and Rebecca with a few soothing words, I eased the bowl carefully on to the stove and sought a match. I watched expectantly as the blue flames licked around the glass bowl. There was as yet no movement. Perhaps I should turn the gas full on? I raised the gas and

13

waited patiently for George and Rebecca's emergence from the ice.

The fish emerged right enough – and so did the ice! They emerged not just from the ice but almost from the house itself. The explosion brought my grandmother almost tumbling down the stairs. I stood in total bewilderment. Where had everything gone? One second there had been two fish, half a gallon of ice and a glass bowl. Now there was only a little pool of water on the top of the gas-stove. I looked slowly around the kitchen. Bits of ice, glass and fish were everywhere.

'You'll cop it when your mum gets in!'

'Nan! I can't find my goldfish!'

'Never mind your soddin' goldfish. Just look at the state of this place. Your mother will have a fit when she sees it!'

I sighed. How typical that was of grown-ups. There I was, attempting to save the lives of two creatures and all I got for it was threats.

Friday evenings at seven differed appreciably from the remainder of the weekdays. Having no school to attend on Saturday, I was allowed to stay up for an extra hour, but, more importantly, it was also bath night. The old galvanized tin bath that spent the rest of the week hanging on a hook in the backyard was now positioned carefully in front of the fire. Another galvanized utensil, this time a bucket, was filled with cold water and placed across two gas-rings. Soon steam would cover everything in the kitchen and rivulets would flow in faltering zig-zag patterns down the window pane. About thirty minutes later, dad would carefully lift the scalding bucket from the gas-stove. The first great steaming splash would hit the bottom of the bath and swirl angrily around as if in search of an occupant. A bucketful of cold water would be added and soon I would be sitting in three inches of warm bath water absolutely reeking of disinfectant and soda. The water that my mother poured with such elegance from a saucepan held immediately above my head had no religious significance at all. It merely indicated to me that my head was about to be covered by great handfuls of Green's Soft Soap. This foul-smelling creation was believed to remove from the skin just about every infestation except ringworm.

A saucepan of rinse; a quick rub down with a stiff towel; and I was almost in a condition where I could be pronounced 'clean'. I say 'almost' because I had yet to receive my laxative, or 'opening medicine' as it was usually called. No working-class bath night was complete without a good purgative. 'Give the boy a thorough clean-out' would be the order of the day. If it ached, blistered or pained, then a good clean-out would cure it. My mother was at least democratic about these laxatives; I could, provided sufficient notice was given, have a choice, that choice being Beecham's Pills, Syrup of Figs or Andrew's Liver Salts. However, when it was realized that I quite liked Liver Salts, they were immediately withdrawn from the list. This decision was made on the premise that if you liked it, then it had to be bad for you.

After supper, with a clean head, clean joints and clean bowels, I would be tucked up in bed all ready to begin the hygienic decline on Saturday morning.

Saturday mornings at 1 Collinson Street were inevitably a time of post mortems. My grandmother would come down and begin to complain to my mother about the latest drunken outrage perpetrated by my grandfather. 'The old man', as he was referred to by everyone (except to his face), was, no doubt, extremely difficult to live with. To say that he enjoyed a pint would be a monumental understatement. He was a navvy by occupation, and he

15

could direct anyone anywhere by the simple process of mentioning public houses. 'You turn right at the King's Arms. Then you keep on till you see a Watney house. Then you turn left, taking the right fork at the William of Orange . . .'

Like most navvies, granddad worked hard and drank harder. But he had once tasted the good life, for a whole month living – as he himself put it – the life of a toff. While excavating during the building of the public toilets in nearby St George's Circus, the walls had collapsed in on him. He was quite seriously injured and for some time lay buried beneath the foundations of the main road. Now cussed though the old man may have been, he was nobody's fool. While he lay fixed in the ground with broken limbs, he took from his pocket his extending steel rule – and began to take measurements! He was eventually rescued and rushed to nearby Guy's Hospital. Later that morning, a policeman called on my grandmother to acquaint her with the old man's injuries. This was an entirely new twist; usually when a policeman called, it was to notify that a surety was required for bail for an offence of drunk and disorderly. Even she felt quite important.

His union decided to fight his case and he was eventually awarded £100 in compensation – about six months' wages. For the old man to be in possession of that sort of money was disastrous. He stopped work and went on a binge that lasted until every penny had gone. This seemed a tragic waste to everyone else, but for the old man it was the highlight of his life.

The strangest thing about granddad was the unquestionable appeal he held for his grandchildren. He could be – as was generally accepted within the family – a real wicked old sod, yet he had a charisma for us kids that was impossible to define. I, for one, thought the absolute world of him. If I happened to be playing in the street on his return home, then, drunk or sober, he would make a great fuss of me. He always carried his spotless pick and shovel, plus a small bundle tied in a red spotted handkerchief. This handkerchief contained the residue of his day's food – nearly always cheese sandwiches. He would place his pick and shovel carefully against the wall, untie his bundle with great reverence, then ceremoniously award me one of his old sandwiches. Invariably they were curly and dry, but they were granddad's sandwiches, and that would make them very special indeed.

The very manner of granddad's arrival in Collinson Street often reflected his financial state. If he was returning home drunk, having spent all his wages in the pub, one clear sign that would always betray him immediately he turned the corner of the street was the sack of 'tarry blocks' that he would be carrying on his shoulders. Most of London's tram-tracks were laid between blocks made of deal and coated with tar, and from time to time they needed to be replaced. Just three of these blocks would keep a family hearth burning brightly for a whole evening; a sackful could keep a complete household warm for a week. This 'navvies' perk' would therefore be offered to granny as a consolation. She may not have received any housekeeping – but at least she had a sackful of blocks!

If Saturday mornings were for family post mortems, then Saturday evenings were for family parties. On that evening, all aunts and uncles returned to the fold and the whole family adjourned to the pub just around the corner. There, in company with numerous other children, I would play at the saloon-bar door of the Winchester public house, having been issued with the statutory glass of lemonade and an Arrowroot biscuit. These biscuits were about the size of pram wheels and slightly less edible: their texture

17

was that of shop-soiled ceiling boards. They were housed in huge glass jars on the pub counter and fished out periodically to act as bribes to the kids that milled around the door.

Once 'time' had been called in the Winchester, the entire family plus a few friends returned to 1 Collinson Street with numerous crates of beer, or occasionally a barrel. The top of my grandmother's piano was then cleared of its vast collection of yellowing stern-faced photographs and the carpet was rolled back. Within minutes a party would be in full swing. A piano was the main ingredient for any decent party, plus of course someone to play it. Anyone who could pick out a tune was in constant demand and plied with free drinks. The result of this obligatory generosity was that around one in the morning the pianist would usually pass out, thus providing the opportunity for any member of the family who fancied themselves as a pianist to step forward. And they did! God but they were awful. Even at that early age, I was amazed at the high level of tolerance shown to such an appalling noise. My own mother was arguably the worst pianist in the entire world. Yet the whole family would be as attentive when she hit, or rather mis-hit, those notes as any Promenade Concert audience listening to Rachmaninov.

If this sounds like the original one-big-happy-family, it wasn't. Frequently the party would end in a fight. Granddad was on the whole indifferent to most of these family brawls, but granny took a different attitude. She was a very small woman, barely five feet tall, but with her shawl, her carpet slippers and her cap, she would take on just about anyone. After one particularly volatile Boxing Day party, Uncle Jim, who lived at West Dulwich, was thrown out. The old lady considered this punishment totally inadequate. The following morning, once my parents had gone to work, she took me on a tram to the wilds of Herne Hill, some four miles away. There she banged continually on Uncle Jim's door. When he finally let us in, she did not bother with any words other than, 'I'll kill you, you bun-house bleeder!' She then launched herself at him with a ferocity that has impressed me for almost half a century. He accepted it as meekly as a lamb. One did not trifle with Emma Ella Shipgood – not when she was wearing her cap, one didn't.

Soon, though, the parties faded. Mum was now heavily pregnant and the opportunity to move house arose: it was to be directly opposite, into Queen's Buildings, an 1870-built gloomy Victorian tenement. The flat consisted of just two rooms with an outside toilet that led off a small balcony. Number 91 was on the fourth floor and was reached via a steep, narrow and damp staircase. While it had roughly the same number of mice as our previous flat, it had a definite increase in bed-bugs.

What, then, could be the attraction of such a move? Well, it had the one thing that mum craved – an amenity that I heard my gran brag about to her friends even before we moved in – it had electricity! Installed and supplied by the Fixed Price Light Company for one shilling and threepence per week and just as much electric light as any family could reasonably need. Who could refuse it? Within days we had made the transition from pavement level to sixty feet up in the sky, with a view far across London's old streets, clear all the way to the cranes at Surrey Docks.

Yet I did not leave the old place without some misgivings. It had one appeal for me that Queen's Buildings could never match. It had a lavatory with a seat that was as wide as the hut itself. This was a tremendous asset. It meant that whenever one of my friends called for me and I happened to be in the lavatory, then they could join me. We could sit side by side and share my comic in a fair degree of comfort. This was an amenity not to be taken lightly, especially when Syrup of Figs had been dispensed with such gusto.

2. Up in the world

The move into Queen's Buildings was fairly easy, except for just one snag – the piano. The driving ambition of most working-class families was to own one, irrespective of whether anyone in the house could actually play the thing. It was a status symbol and a conversation piece. Well, my mother's two office-cleaning jobs had finally paid dividends and we could now afford one ourselves: a fine, upright, polished-like-glass Barnes piano. But how does one take a piano up to the fourth floor of Queen's Buildings? Well, certainly not easily. Definitely not via the staircase, it was far too narrow and, in any case, the landing corners were much too sharp.

'I'll tell you what we'll do,' said the delivery men. 'We'll take it in through the window.'

As archaic as the old dwellings were, at the front they sported rather generous windows. (The back of the buildings was a very different matter: there the lights had to be kept on all day.) The front window frame was removed and the cooperation of the family in the flat above was sought. A block and tackle was installed on the fifth floor and the ropes were lowered to ground level. The piano, looking anything but safe, was then partially wrapped in a canvas sheet and bound with two thick ropes.

'Stand clear down there!' came the message from on high, then, with a series of faltering jerks, the package slowly began its ascent. Below, a lip-biting crowd waited

21

expectantly for a disaster. What a sight that would be! A piano that crashed down four floors on to the pavement! Every kid in the school would want to talk to me. But, sadly, no matter how much I wished and crossed my fingers, it just wasn't to be. The only hitch came at the moment when the two delivery men presented my mother with the bill. 'Ten shillings!' she exploded. 'It's a bloody robbery!'

With the siting of the piano, we had finally completed the move into Queen's Buildings. Mum and dad slept in the front room with all the best furniture, and I slept in a corner of the kitchen with a ceiling-to-floor curtain draped around my bed. I quite enjoyed the position of that bed because it meant I could eavesdrop on all the family news. Front rooms were hardly ever used in those days, and any discussion between family, friends or callers always took place in the kitchen. My bed being so well draped, no one knew if I was asleep or awake, and I used to lie there, fascinated, listening to all the confidential talk.

This was not without its dangers. One evening, after my grandfather had behaved particularly outrageously, my grandmother arrived at our door and confided to my mother her wishes for the old man's future, 'I'll do him in, I swear I will, I'll swing for the sod!' being just about the mildest of her desires. My mother consoled her with lashings of sympathy and gradually she quietened down. This seemed quite unfair to me. How could they sit there and be so unkind to my grandfather? He was a lovely old chap. He had a warm, beery, tobacco-ey smell and he always gave away his sandwiches. No one could be kinder. With all the maturity of a six-year-old, I decided that something had to be done. The following afternoon, on a tea-time visit across the road to 1 Collinson Street, I told the old man everything that had been said about him.

Just what sort of upheaval that caused in my

grandparents' household I never discovered. I was too busy sheltering from the rain of blows being inflicted by my avenging mother. I ran for protection to the big old armchair that was the old man's throne. Granddad would shelter me, he would stop that cane from crashing across the various parts of my anatomy. But the old man was too drunk to offer more than a token – 'Why don't you (burp) leave the boy alone (burp).' Then he slumped back into the chair and fell asleep. That incident saw my first disillusionment with the kindly old man whom I had always worshipped.

A few weeks later I was awoken early one Saturday morning by my father. He whispered that I was to dress quickly because I was about to go and stay with my Aunt Lylie and Uncle Tim for a few days. I was, it seems, about to have a brother – or a sister. Whatever its sex, it obviously did not wish for me to be around when it arrived. I quite enjoyed the hustle and bustle that was suddenly taking place all around me. A fat lady whom I had never seen before kept putting her head out of our front room and telling me to hurry up.

'Can I take Pie-Shop?'

'No, you can't. Your aunt already has a dog and they'll fight.'

'But Pie-Shop won't fight,' I protested. 'He's too windy.' (He may have been my dog and I loved him, but I was under no illusions about his courage.)

It was no use. Within a few minutes I was being escorted by my dad to my Aunt Lylie's, just a few streets away. It felt really good to have dad around on a Saturday morning. The long hours that he usually spent at the factory meant that I saw comparatively little of him. He had always left for work before I woke and he usually arrived home only shortly before I went to bed. Even Saturdays were no

23

improvement. He would work at the factory until 1.30 p.m. and probably play football until late afternoon.

Five minutes later we had reached my aunt's address and climbed the fifty or so stairs to her attic flat. Leaving me in her good care, dad hurried back to Queen's Buildings.

Although I had been deprived of Pie-Shop, I did have a chance to renew my friendship with the far more dependable Joe. 'Old Joe', as he was more commonly called, was an old English sheepdog that my Uncle Tim used on his coal round. Tim and his dog were quite a feature of the neighbourhood. When my uncle reached up to the back of the cart to remove the hundredweight sacks of coal, so Old Joe would push the bag from the opposite side. Joe was a huge muscular dog on whose back I had frequently ridden when I was very young.

It was a lovely weekend. I was allowed to brush the coaldust from Joe's thick coat and attend the stables with Uncle Tim on Sunday, in order to groom and feed his carthorse. Seeing the animal standing in his stable gave me my first impression of an animal's absolute power. I had often watched Prince between the shafts of the cart, but this was the first time that I had seen the creature unshackled. He looked immense. While I admired the huge animal, I was also intimidated by his sheer physical presence. During that afternoon, Aunt Ly told me that I had a 'brand new brother', and his name was to be Stanley Eric. I was obviously expected to be impressed. Well, I wasn't.

However, the arrival of my brother instantly changed my status and I could not have been more pleased about this. No longer the baby of the house, I was able to enjoy a great deal more freedom. I was eager to break away from the confines of the three or four streets immediately around Queen's Buildings; in particular, I longed to go down to the river, some half a mile away. On the whole, children of inner London were very parochial and half a mile was considered to be a fair distance. Among my first discoveries on one of these unsupervised excursions was Bella White's.

The notorious Mrs White allegedly ran 'a house' which all sorts of ladies frequented. The alley in which her gloomy house stood was known locally as Horny Lane. (At six years of age the subtlety of this title was somewhat lost on me.) It was said that if Bella White ever saw a child loitering anywhere near her house, she would leap out on them, drug them and drag them in. Once she had you inside the premises, she would either chop you up and put you into pies, or occasionally – and I suppose this was done for pure variety – she'd cut off your willie. The spreading of this story – and half the kids at my school swore they knew at least three of the victims – had, for the dubious Mrs White, one very useful advantage. It ensured that disturbances from children were kept to an absolute minimum, with small boys being positively angelic. On the other hand, some sort of opposition to this butchery had to be found. Resistance manifested itself in a ditty that was usually chanted from the corner of her alley just before running like hell for home. The words went thus:

> Down Horny Lane, there are some dirty women
> And if you want to see them, you'll have to pay a shilling.
> Soldiers half a crown; sailors half a guinea;
> Big fat men, two pounds ten,
> Little boys, a penny.

Now I must have been a very fair-minded child indeed, because I remember it really offended my sense of justice that sailors were expected to spend half a guinea. I had always wanted to be a sailor and it seemed outrageous that sailors should pay out four times as much as soldiers, just for the privilege of seeing a dirty woman. In any case, I was never really sure just what dirty women were. Mum had always said that it was very dirty to have a candle running down from your nose. And how about Rosie Pilbeam? She had nits! Mum said nits were dirty too. Would sailors be expected to pay half a guinea to see the fair Rosie's nits? If you sat next to her at school for more than twenty minutes they would leap out all over you for nothing. No, there were definitely puzzling aspects to Bella White's, not the least of these being the fact that I never once saw her and I was not even sure which house in Horny Lane she lived in.

This newfound freedom to roam was not without its drawbacks, the biggest being errand-running. Oh, how I hated running errands, and it wasn't helped by the sixty-four stairs that had to be climbed every time. It was bad enough that I should have to run them for mum and occasionally gran, but now in the Buildings there was old Mrs Morton to contend with. Mrs Morton lived underneath us at number 89 together with her three grown-up children. She was a lovely old dear but her ability to hear me pass by her door used to send me mad. I never knew how she did it. Her front door would be closed, with a blanket draped inside it to keep out the draught. I would tip-toe the two flights of stairs that preceded her door and also the two flights past it, yet she never once failed to hear my stealthy footsteps. Her 'order' was usually the same: "Allo, Ginge-boy,' she would say, opening her door at the exact moment I was creeping past. 'Go an' get me 'alf-ounce-a-Wilsons. There's a good lad.'

'Wilsons' was a particularly odious form of snuff which made me sneeze with a series of neck-cracking jerks. The bespectacled, white-aproned shopowner would carefully spoon the fine-grained powder on to his shiny brass scales. Then he would weigh it as meticulously as if it were gold dust. Slowly the scales tilted as a few precious grains evened up the balance. At this stage he would peer at me over the top of his spectacles, as if daring me to sneeze and blow the whole lot away. Then he would pick up the dish off the scales with infinite care and smoothly tilt the contents into a small piece of paper. Finally, with a deft twist he would lift the edges and secure them into a dolly-like twirl. 'Twopence,' he would say as he thrust the tiny package deliberately under my nose. Firing several staccato sneezes, I would drop the two pennies in his open palm and run.

Just occasionally there would be a variation in Mrs Morton's shopping list. If it wasn't snuff that I was required to purchase then it would almost certainly be a gas-mantle. Although Queen's Buildings had been wired for electric light, a great number of families still preferred gaslight, due to the illogical belief that should anything go wrong, 'Well, you can always smell gas, can't you, but you can't smell electricity.' The trouble with gas-mantles was that they were so confoundedly fragile. About the size of a large egg cup and packed in small, square cardboard boxes, they appeared to be made of a stiff but extremely delicate gauze. For maximum safety they needed to be treated like nitroglycerine. The slightest jar and they would crumble into a thousand pieces. Gas-mantles and small boys were not compatible, they never could be. More errand-running kids were bashed over the subject of gas-mantles than over any other single item.

The other pet hate was accumulator-changing. Accumulators looked like square jam-jars, were full of acid and bubbled continuously. Every battery-operated radio set needed one, and every ten to twelve days they had to

27

be replaced. On every few streets there would be shops where for twopence or threepence these jars could be exchanged. Each evening at these shops there would be an endless procession of kids, carefully clutching their effervescent acid-jars. One of the advantages of living at Queen's Buildings was that my accumulator-running was nowhere near as bad as it might have been. Although my grandmother and Mrs Morton still used the old battery wireless sets, mum and dad were now in possession of a brand new electric radio. This had but one disadvantage. Under the terms of the Fixed Price Light Company no electric apparatus other than two sixty-watt bulbs was permitted to be used in any one flat. An electrician friend of the family had fixed the new radio into the kitchen light socket. This functioned quite well, but it meant that whenever there was an unexpected knock on the door the whole apparatus had to be dismantled just in case it was a caller from the Fixed Price Light Company. Such was progress.

Of course not all errand-running would be grounds for despair. Some errands were quite pleasant and rewarding, none more so than a trip to the baker's. In any hundred-yard journey from the shop to his front door, an average small boy could pull out and consume half the contents of a large crusty loaf. Long before I had climbed those sixty-four stairs to our flat, my hand would be wrist-deep into any 'long crusty'. Most kids could expect to receive a clump around the ear on returning home with a good third of the family loaf missing, yet it was considered a risk well worth taking. I would have chanced it just for the smell.

My career as an errand runner, along with the life of Pie-Shop, almost had an early finish. Having been told to fetch fish and chips one Friday lunchtime, I asked my mother if I could take Pie-Shop along with me. 'Well, all right, but

– only if you take him on a lead, then,' she replied reluctantly. 'That road is really very busy and he might cause an accident,' she added, prophetically.

Some fifteen minutes later I stood on the pavement outside Old Lew's fried fish shop waiting for the traffic to clear. Clutching two hot portions of fish and chips under one arm, I was restraining Pie-Shop with the other. Suddenly he gave an extra jerk that tipped me into the road and I staggered forward a couple of paces, still trying very hard to hold on to our hot dinners. I will say one thing for that dog – he had style. There were lorries, horse-drawn carts and trams in abundance all travelling that Friday lunchtime along Southwark Bridge Road. There was even the occasional private car. But with a divine sense of the big occasion, Pie-Shop picked out a fire-engine! As the dog disappeared under its huge wheels, I was knocked some feet into the air and I came down semi-dazed on the tram-line. As my bare legs struck the cold metal of the lines, my street instinct immediately told me that this was no place to hang about. I clambered to my feet and ran across the remainder of the road, running and falling, running and falling, oblivious to the rest of the traffic. Only when I had reached the sanctuary of the opposite kerb did I stop to look around. The sight was pretty confusing. The fire-engine had halted at a strange angle to the kerb and a cyclist was disentangling himself from the bent frame of his machine, presumably having run into the back of the fire-engine. Two white-faced firemen were running towards me while a third was assisting the cyclist. My first instinct was to turn and dash for home. I was suddenly aware that my left arm was being tugged. Looking down, I was astonished to see Pie-Shop still on his lead and apparently unharmed. Amazingly, I was still in possession of both the dog and the fish and chips!

'Are you all right, sonny?' the first of the firemen anxiously enquired.

'All right?' I thought. 'Yes, why shouldn't I be?' Suddenly the penny dropped. I had just been knocked down – *and* by a fire-engine! Bloody hell! Wouldn't that impress them at school!

'Look, he's bleeding!' said the second fireman as he pointed to my legs. A trickle of blood had begun to make its way from underneath the bottoms of my short trousers. 'Where are you hurt, son?'

The glamour was fading rapidly. I was not averse to being knocked down but I had no desire to be hurt! I started to cry. Pie-Shop jumped up and began to lick my face as the fireman picked me up and carried me back to the fish shop. A sea of faces surrounded me and I could hear dramatic whispers being uttered. 'He's bleeding internally.' I had no idea what 'internally' meant but it didn't sound good. I cried even harder.

'Where d'you live, son?' said the second fireman.

I told him, and yet another member of the fire-crew ran off to tell my mother.

'Can you give her these fish and chips?' I called after him, anxious to relieve myself of at least some of my burden, but he showed no great interest in my request.

The grease had now penetrated the paper and bits of crushed fish and chips were beginning to spill out everywhere. Someone removed the greasy package from me, and next to appear was an ambulance man. After a few quiet words with the fireman, he carefully removed my trousers and gave me a quick examination.

'You'll be all right, Ginger, you've only got a cut bum. A couple of stitches and you'll be as good as new.'

A cut bum! Well, that wasn't very good. I wanted to go to school swathed in bandages. It didn't matter how much bandage you had around your bum, no one was likely to see it there.

'Well, er, my arm hurts a bit,' I offered.

'I think that's only a bruise, Ginger lad,' replied the ambulance man. 'But the doctor'll have a look when we get to the hospital. Can you walk?'

I struggled manfully to my feet. 'How about Pie-Shop?'

'Pie-Shop?'

'Pie-Shop, my dog, of course. Can I take him with me?'

'Not in the ambulance, you can't.'

'I'll look after him,' said Old Lew, the shop's owner, making his first contribution to the proceedings.

A few minutes later, I lay on my belly with my chin on my hands and my bare bum exposed in a cubicle in Evelina Children's Hospital, just a quarter of a mile down the road. A rustling-starched, soap-smelling nurse dabbed confidently at my backside with tufts of stinging cotton wool. She kept up a constant chatter. Where do you live? How old are you? Where d'you go to school? What's your dog's name? And all very boring questions like that.

'Will I have a very big bandage?' I asked hopefully.

'Oh, I shouldn't think so,' she answered matter-of-factly. 'It's only a little cut. I should think just a plaster will be fine.'

'Oh.'

'Would you like a bandage, then?'

'Yes, please!' I answered eagerly.

She smiled. 'Well, perhaps we'll see what we can do for you.' A doctor then entered the cubicle and repeated the very same questions that I had just answered for the nurse. 'I'm going to put three stitches in your bottom,' he explained. 'You'll just feel a few small pin-pricks and then you can go home. Your mother is waiting outside for you.'

'Oh, doctor,' interrupted the nurse, 'I think he would

like a bandage. He does have a bruise on his arm.' She pointed to the arm and smiled again.

Some fifteen minutes later, the doctor led me to the waiting-room and reunited me with my mother. Gran was also with her. My only visible sign of injury was a wide bandage on my left arm. My shirt sleeve was rolled up just as far as I could get it, showing the bandage to its maximum effect. Mum made quite a fuss of me but spoilt it all by announcing it was the last time that I could take Pie-Shop out on an errand. I felt that her reasoning was all wrong. It wasn't the dog that had caused the accident, it was the bloody errand. Surely anyone could see that?

3. Hands, nits, naughty bits

Charles Dickens Junior Mixed School, near London Bridge, was built in 1877, seven years after the writer's early death. It reeked of radiator-warmed milk, wet knickers and dirty ink-wells. Many of Dickens's characters either originated in the immediate area or subsequently gravitated there, and several of the area's shadier spots are described in his novels. At the age of twelve, Dickens had himself worked in the next street in a blacking factory, in an attempt to raise enough money to secure his father's release from a debtor's prison. Certainly up until the 1930s the whole area reeked of Dickens. Some sixty years after his death, even though probably fewer than a handful of local people had actually read a Dickens book, the names of many of his characters were in everyday usage.

Take Sarah Gamp, for example. She may have featured in *Martin Chuzzlewit* but she also had a shellfish stall outside the Winchester public house. It was there, my father claimed, that she regularly urinated over the cockles and whelks. With her gin-rimmed eyes, red nose and dubious habits of hygiene, she bore an astonishing resemblance to the literary character. Mr Quilp also had other functions besides frightening the daylights out of Little Nell and her senile old grandfather in *The Old Curiosity Shop*. He had a pawnshop to manage in Southwark Bridge Road. And as for the Artful Dodger – well, Queen's Buildings had dozens. Even the staff at

Charles Dickens school did their best to emulate some of these characters. Take Miss Atkins the headmistress, for example. She was the ultimate figure of authority. She strode through classrooms, playground and halls like the epitome of Victorian discipline, the school keys that she kept linked to her belt rattling out a sinister warning of her approach. Daily she would rap my knuckles to discourage me from writing with my left hand.

If Miss Atkins was like a workhouse master, then Miss (Fanny) Potter was the Beadle. She would echo all of Miss Atkins's decrees and wallop us at will. Or at least she did until the day she bent forward to tan the backside of some seven-year-old delinquent. His struggling resentment made her wig fall off into the bucket of chalky water that was kept to wash down the blackboard. Her dignity in tatters and her secret exposed, she snatched up her dripping wet toupée and ran tearfully from the room. For a few delirious minutes supreme anarchy reigned in the classroom. Suddenly the distant sound of keys could be heard rattling ever closer. By the time the door opened, the silence in the classroom was overpowering. Miss Atkins said nothing. She simply strode to the centre of the classroom and, with hands on hips, glared all around. Not a face was prepared to meet hers. Heads were kept down and eyes were kept shut. 'I should think so too,' she hissed, in a whisper that cut into every recess of the school. As if in punishment for Fanny Potter's misfortune, Miss Atkins stayed in our classroom for the rest of the day. It was so quiet that I felt guilty when I breathed.

All was not gloom, however. After the departure of Miss Potter we had in Miss Helen Jones a female version of Samuel Pickwick. The whole class loved her. Her enthusiasm carried us all along in every project the class undertook. With this Pickwickian club attitude she would make sums as interesting as any Christmas pantomime.

Finally there was Mrs Bonney, the stern school nurse. Periodically we would line up in the hall in true workhouse style to have our heads searched for nits. Our heads bowed, Mrs Bonney would rummage diligently with a metal comb and drag it in a determined search for 'lodgers'. Were any found, the victim would be whisked away to the cleansing station where he or she was bathed and shampooed and their clothing baked. The boys would also sustain a ferocious twopenny-all-off-haircut which resulted in a brush-like appearance, no strand of hair measuring more than half an inch.

Looking for nits was not the only function of the redoubtable Mrs Bonney, her full brief being 'hands, nits and naughty bits'. Diseases like impetigo, for example, caused great concern. A small outbreak could spread round a school like the plague. Any sore on the body was instantly investigated. Great dabs of Gentian Violet would leave the recipient looking like a woad-covered ancient Briton. For obvious reasons, Mrs Bonney was always referred to by the children formally as 'the nitty-nurse', or, informally, Nitty-Nora. It never really dawned on me that she actually had any other name, that is until the day she sent me with a message to my teacher, Miss Jones.

'Miss, miss!' I blurted out rather urgently. 'The nitty-nurse wants to see you.'

The lovely Miss Jones turned to me and sighed. 'Will you please try to remember that Mrs Bonney does not *nurse* nits – quite the reverse, in fact!'

At the age of seven, children were transferred from 'The Infants' to 'The Juniors'. There we were to remain until the eleventh-year examination sorted out the academics from the duffers. Each class kept its same teacher; in fact the only difference I found was that the playground games became tougher. The playground bullies began to emerge but the school code of 'not telling Miss' ensured their survival. This code decreed that no one informed, no matter how great their tribulation. The result was that many children went to school in total dread. If their tormentor also lived in the same street, then that dread could continue through all of their waking hours. Fortunately for me, I did not suffer from these horrors. Instead I was able to pursue my three main playtime interests: football, cricket and girls, approximately in that order. Not, I hasten to add, that I pursued girls in any sexual capacity, it was more out of pure curiosity.

While the boys chased balls around and bashed each other, girls would tuck their skirts into their navy-blue knickers (they were *always* navy-blue) and 'go up the wall', which simply meant doing a handstand against a wall. I always considered this to be one of the most pointless exercises of all time. Yet dozens of girls, scattered all around the playground, would regularly participate in it. God only knew why. These gymnastics would be done on such a scale that for some considerable time I thought the main difference between the two sexes was that boys were just – well, boys. Girls, on the other hand, were always upside down and wore navy-blue drawers.

Every Friday morning exams based on the week's work were held. Miss Jones would mark the papers at lunch-time and the first item of the afternoon would be the results. The position in which one sat in class would depend entirely on these results. The desks were arranged as in a league table, with four rows running from the front of the class to the back. Highest marks in the exam would allow the winner to sit at the front and on Miss Jones's extreme right. There were two children to a desk, therefore the runner-up would be next to the winner. The third in the list would be in the second row of desks immediately behind the winner and so on. In this way whenever Miss Atkins entered any class she could see at a glance the academic position of every child in the room.

The main complainer about this grading system was my mother, not for any academic reason but solely because I was the mental equivalent of Rose Pilbeam. Now I very much enjoyed Rosie's company and she was always capable of making me giggle in class. However there was absolutely no doubt that Rosie – sweetie though she was – was usually running-alive-lousy.

'How did you get on in the exam today?' mum would anxiously ask every Friday evening.

'Oh, er, all right, I s'pose, mum.'

'How many marks did you get?'

I hated this follow-up question. It was much too precise for comfort.

'Oh, well, I don't actually know how many marks I got – but it was quite a lot.' The cheerfulness of my tone was always painfully false.

'How many did Rosie Pilbeam get?'

'Er, same as me, mum.'

This would be the signal for me to be grabbed and dragged to the kitchen table. There I would be seated with my head bent forward over a newspaper that was laid out on the table. A fine dog-comb would appear and Mum would drag it forward across my scalp in a series of tugging sweeps. Woe betide me if anything fell out on to the newspaper. 'Ah-ha! There's one!' A finger would be pressed down on the tiny body and a faint crack would be heard.

The tension that my mother experienced each Friday night built up to a climax a few days before our Christmas school pantomime. Together with five other classmates, I was to be a guardsman in a Christopher Robin and Alice sketch. Miss Atkins had suggested that each of us might care to come to school that day in a guardsman's-red jersey. Miss Atkins's suggestions carried all the authority of a royal decree.

'I've got to have a red jersey for school, mum.'

'Why?'

'Cos Miss Atkins says so.'

'I don't care *what* Miss Atkins says. You don't possess a red jersey and I can't afford to buy you one.'

'But Miss Atkins *says* so, mum, she *says* so!' I emphasized. Why was it, I wondered, that grown-ups could never understand the compulsion of Miss Atkins's 'saying so'.

After several days of tears and pleading, my mother eventually relented. But unfortunately the jersey that she purchased was more crimson than red. It may have pleased me – and to a lesser extent my mother – but it did not please Miss Cynthia Atkins, not in the least it didn't. On the morning of the play at our final rehearsal, Miss Atkins noticed that Rosie Pilbeam was wearing her brother Billy's old red jersey. Well, yes, it was old, and yes, it was none too clean, but it was *red*. For Miss Atkins that was good enough.

'Right, change jumpers, you two!'

I must confess that I never gave the swop a moment's thought. It seemed such a good idea. After all, if I was now wearing a proper guardsman's-red jumper, then who could complain? Certainly not me.

The rehearsal rumbled along to a finish and soon the first of the mums were assembling in the school hall. Just before the curtain was due to part for the grand opening, six little guardsmen filed self-consciously on to the stage. Because of the lack of space, we six were to stand in front of the curtain until it parted. Miss Jones, who was sitting at the school piano, began to pick out the first few bars of 'They're changing guard at Buckingham Palace . . .' The spotlight came on and the old blue curtain was swished back. Christopher Robin opened his mouth to sing.

'Harry!' came mum's voice, cutting up from three rows back. 'Where is your jersey?' Every word was as hard as an icicle.

'Er, Rosie's got it, mum.'

'Rosie? Well, whose jersey have you got on?'

'Well, er, Rosie's. Or it might be Billy's,' I added, none too optimistically.

'Rosie or B – !!'

Chairs scattered as mum crashed through the assembled audience. She reached up on to the stage and dragged me by the neck of the offending garment, down into the front row. No guard had ever been changed quicker. Christopher Robin and Alice were astonished. Mum hurled the jersey with as much force as she could muster in the general direction of Miss Atkins.

'How dare you, you wicked old bitch! How dare you!' she screamed at the astonished headmistress.

Poor Rosie, having read the situation only too clearly, was already peeling off my jersey and exposing her extremely grimy liberty-bodice to a totally unappreciative audience. Mum snatched up the crimson jersey and held it at arm's length. Then, holding me at an almost equal distance with the other arm, she swept out of the now crowded hall.

I lay long awake that night wondering just what Miss Atkins's reaction would be. There was to be no easy way out for me. Mum made it quite clear that there was to be no question of me missing school that day. In fact she had arrived home early from work in order to deliver me to

39

school on time. Gripping my hand tightly, she bustled my reluctant legs in the direction of the playground. The mid-December fog seemed to close in in sympathy.

The daily register was called and a few minutes later, the classes began to file into the assembly hall. Miss Atkins stood motionless on the small raised dais at the far end of the hall. Her gaze ran expertly down each arriving class. I felt it stop when it reached me. Apparently satisfied with her observations, she appeared to show no further interest in the proceedings. Heads were bowed and hands were clasped as Miss Topham, the deputy headmistress, led us all in the morning prayer. Miss Jones then played the final hymn, and, in the normal course of events, that would have been the finish of assembly. Suddenly Miss Atkins stepped forward once again.

'Harry Cole and Rose Pilbeam, stay behind after assembly. Thank you.'

I felt the centre fall out of my bum.

The last of the children left the hall and the headmistress sat at the now empty piano busying herself with some correspondence. Rosie and I glanced anxiously at each other. After a couple of minutes Miss Atkins looked up and, for the first time that I could remember, she smiled!

'Rosie, how would you and Harry like to be ink-monitors next term?'

Ink-monitors! Cor, wouldn't we! 'Yes, miss, yes. Thanks a lot!' we chorused.

Well, I couldn't see how mum could mind me working with Rosie if I was ink-monitor. But just to be on the safe side, I never mentioned it.

4. Games and gangs

The gradual transition of brother Stan from a baby into a toddler presented me with two problems. First, he was transferred from his cot in the front room to share my bed in the kitchen. This was a small problem and I quickly, albeit reluctantly, adapted. The second problem was far more difficult to overcome. From time to time I would be expected to take Stan out in the street in his pram and there be responsible for him. It is true that this only happened a couple of times a week, but oh how I hated it! However, after a while I discovered that this new responsibility did have definite advantages. Stan was gradually becoming very much in demand among other children in the street. At first I just shoved his pram against the wall and tried to forget about him. But whenever I did this, I discovered that there were at least four doll-less girls who would practically fight over him. Well, if they wanted him, they could have him! Once mum had begun to climb those stairs and was out of sight, I would instantly delegate responsibility. This enabled me to get on with the more serious childhood activities such as jumping on the backs of lorries.

Stealing rides was probably the most popular sport among young boys at that time. In theory this activity was very dangerous but in practice it was enormous fun. Two or three boys would wait at a junction or a set of traffic lights until a suitable open-backed lorry stopped. Then, as the truck moved away and gathered speed, they would rush out into the road and leap up to grab the tailboard of the now fast departing vehicle. Each boy would then have to use his own judgement of the best moment to drop off. The last one to let go was considered the winner. A late decision by the participant would often result in him losing his balance and toppling head-first into the road. This was considered to be unskilful but it was usually accepted, however grudgingly, as a result. There was just the finest of dividing lines between a 'late decision' and blind terror. This sometimes caused a nervous child to remain hanging from the tailboard as it roared out of sight around the distant bend of Southwark Bridge Road. This rather negative approach was an automatic disqualification. The shame-faced contestant would usually arrive back on foot some thirty minutes later, having walked anything up to two miles.

A far less dangerous form of joy-riding could be carried out on the backs of horse-drawn carts. These vehicles, being much slower than the lorries, were in one sense easier targets. They did, however, present a very big drawback – the driver's whip! While a lorry driver could do little to shake off any young tailboard-hanger, except accelerate and brake sharply, the horse-driver, or carter as he was known, was much better equipped to rid himself of the hanger-on, by virtue of his whip. The little white knuckles of a novice joy-rider, peeping just above the tailboard, presented a challenging target that few carters could resist – or miss. A sharp crack would be followed by an even sharper pain and the bewildered boy would find himself dumped in the road with his fingers throbbing. The old cart meanwhile would rumble cheerfully away down the street.

Great road-safety campaigns were directed against this joy-riding practice. Slides were shown in school, lectures given and bottoms tanned. A boy seen anywhere near the rear of a vehicle would almost certainly receive a thump. Everyone from the headmistress to the school cleaner drummed into our heads the danger of running behind lorries. We listened with revered attention and agreed with everything that was said. Then, on leaving school for the day, we would of course jump on the first lorry that was passing.

Although my brother Stan was much too young for the backs of lorries, he was not without his own share of road dangers. Whenever he could be pried away from his female admirers, he, together with his pram, was in demand as a stage-coach. Prams of course make excellent stage-coaches. The usual practice was for two boys to run along Collinson Street towing the pram at high speed. These two gallant steeds would then be brutally shot down by crooked cowboys or renegade Indians. The two poor victims would then tumble dramatically to the ground, leaving the stage-coach to roar on totally out of control. Most stage-coaches would in those circumstances either hit a boulder and disintegrate, or fall into a deadly ravine, preferably one infested with poisonous snakes. Queen's Buildings was sadly lacking in all of these obstacles, therefore we had to make do with the kerbstones.

My personal preference for the place of ultimate destruction of any stage-coach was the river. A really good crash into the river had the essential air of finality about it. Sadly, mum had decidedly strong views about taking the pram anywhere near the Thames. This was a great pity because we never did discover if the thing could float. However the question was partially resolved when Bill Pilbeam pointed out that Southwark Bridge Road, which ran as 'T' junction across the western end of Collinson Street, was probably the same width as many of the rivers in cowboy films. Now Billy was never the brightest member of our group, so we had to admit that he had really excelled himself in this project. With a little imagination, Southwark Bridge Road could indeed be easily mistaken for just about any river in South Dakota. This, then, was the answer. Instead of running the pram blindly into the kerb, we could run it equally blindly into Southwark Bridge Road.

Surprisingly, the child lived, although in retrospect I cannot understand why. Stan, of course, absolutely loved it. He would be catapulted driverless into the main-road traffic, chuckling away deliriously as hooting cars and lorries swerved all around him. When he finally crashed into the kerbstones on the opposite side of the road, his peals of laughter could be heard the whole length of Collinson Street. This marvellous game, which became increasingly popular, was eventually stopped by a humourless neighbour who told my mother of the precarious existence of her baby.

Stan's enforced departure from my playtime scene did not upset me much. A whole new world was opening up for me and I was bursting to explore it. This world was all of one square mile in size but it seemed absolutely enormous. The river was probably the greatest of the lures. There were just so many things to see and do there. Endless processions of tugs and steamers would throb their way up and down the Thames. Often these craft appeared to be much too big to negotiate the low clearances of many of the Thames bridges. Great colliers belonging to the Gas Light and Coke Company would determinedly plough their way through the waters on an apparent collision course with the centre spans of Southwark Bridge. Then, just yards from seeming disaster, the smoking black funnel would hinge back and lie flat along the deck of the boat. For any kid leaning precariously over the parapet of the bridge, this would mean a lungful of smoke and a faceful of soot. A small price to pay for so rewarding a sight. Rubbish boats, sludge boats, dredgers and barges, all would crowd the grimy Thames. I would sit for hours on the Bankside wall just dreaming of the day when I was grown up and could work on the river.

Lines of these great fat barges would be moored six deep on the shiny black mudflats alongside the river walls. By climbing the wall and swinging across the ropes that secured each barge, we would eventually gain access to the furthermost line. Playing on those particular craft gave a splendid feeling of isolation and achievement. We seemed so far away from the shore that at high tide we could pretend we were at sea.

Just occasionally disaster would strike. Barges and the stinking mud were the greatest hazards. Whenever a boy was crushed by a barge, or trapped by the mud, no child would be seen on that section of the river for days. Yet within a week all would be back, each claiming to have been present at the ''orrible death' or, at the very least, to have been the best mate of the deceased.

The victim of one accident, however, was envied by us all. During one drizzling school holiday a group of us managed to drop down into the furthermost empty barge. We spent some hours there sheltering from the rain before pangs of hunger prompted our return home. As one by one we leapt from the barge, we became aware that the craft had moved. This was not unusual – the moving tides would often cause the floating barges to settle, or occasionally bump into a neighbouring barge – but this time the gap between the two barges was widening alarmingly. Everyone on board finally jumped clear except for Charlie Martin. Charlie was quite fat and certainly not as quick on his feet as the rest of us. The two ropes that should have secured the barge hung limply down into the water as the hulk swung oh-so-calmly out into the mainstream of the Thames. The gap was probably just too wide for Charlie to jump but the barge was now almost stationary, just a couple of yards from us and tantalizingly out of reach.

'Come on, Charlie, jump!' we yelled.

Charlie faltered. Each passing second made him more indecisive. One problem was that there was very little room for a decent run-up. However, he backed away just as far as he could and rocked quickly backwards and forwards, as if preparing himself for some gargantuan effort. With his teeth clenched hard, his fat face began to rock in unison with the rest of his body. We all knew that Charlie would never make it and were quite enjoying the prospect of watching him falling in the river. You never know – he might drown.

Charlie released his body from its coiled-spring posture and hurled himself towards the gap between the boats. About thirty inches away from it he changed his mind. His feet stopped easily enough. His difficulty came when the weight of his body finally overtook his legs. Then Charlie really did have a problem. As he bent forward almost double, both of his arms came up from behind him and began to whirr like aeroplane propellers. Charlie stayed in that position for what seemed like ages. Suddenly he fell forwards and clutched at one of the great ropes that trailed from the barge down into the water. The truth then finally hit us. Charlie was not going to fall into the river after all! Breathlessly he pulled himself up to a sitting position.

'That was all your faults, that was,' he panted. His bottom lip quivered and he burst into tears.

'Oy, you kids! What're you doing of down there?' came a voice from on high. We all looked up to see an inquisitive face peering out of the driver's cabin of a nearby crane.

Sensibly thinking that we would be blamed whatever the cause, Rosie Pilbeam yelled, 'Run!' It seemed like one of Rosie's better ideas and we were away like rabbits.

We breathlessly reassembled some minutes later at the bottom of our stairs in Queen's Buildings. My first reaction was one of shame for deserting poor Charlie. But Rosie soon made me feel a whole lot better.

'Serve 'im right,' she said. ''E shouldn't 'ave been so fat.'

Now, of course, we were faced with another problem. How do we tell Charlie's mum that her only child is the sole castaway on a runaway barge? In reality the problem was easily solved – we simply forgot about it. Or, more accurately, we forgot about it until the next morning when Charlie's picture appeared in one of the newspapers after his rescue by the Thames Police. 'Child Cast Away By Hooligans,' said the headline.

''Ere, Charlie's famous,' said Rosie.

'If we'd stayed on the barge we'd 'ave been famous too,' said Billy ruefully.

We never did find out who slipped the ropes of that barge. But if Charlie had not looked quite so terror-struck when we left him on board, he would have been my prime suspect.

I was now at an age when I could be accepted into the street gang. There was no rigid or clear-cut starting age but I was growing fast and a boy would simply evolve into the group. Each street, or occasionally two small streets, would have its own gang. Queen's Buildings, situated as it was across some five streets, could have produced a very powerful gang indeed. Yet strangely enough its adolescent population preferred to divide itself among the smaller street gangs. On the whole these were neither violent nor criminal and often sported quite strict codes of conduct. Any fight between members, for instance, was considered finished the moment one of the protagonists fell to the ground. Kicking and girls were taboo and anyone wearing spectacles was as safe as a mother superior – that is, providing he did not push his luck too far.

Probably the most feared gang in the whole area was the 'Red Cross Way mob'. Red Cross Way consisted mainly of a large block of nearby tenements that had achieved the solidarity which always eluded Queen's Buildings. Wildly exaggerated stories about the behaviour of Red Cross Way would race through the street grapevine. Fortunately for us, we were on very good terms with them and they assisted us on many occasions. It was amazing how brave you could be when you knew that the Red Cross Way gang were on your side. If only 5 per cent of the stories about them were true, then they made the hordes of the Hun look like the Primrose League.

The melting pot for the street gangs was the Saturday morning cinemas. There all rivalries were forgotten as we cheered Flash Gordon and booed Emperor Ming to the echo. The local cinema for Queen's Buildings was a real fleapit that went under the oddly religious name of The Trinity. It was The Trinity that made me first aware of the unacceptable face of capitalism. Overnight it changed its name from The Trinity to The Royalty, the flag-pole was painted and the price of admission increased from twopence to threepence.

There were always two very important things to remember at The Trinity. (Every kid refused on principle to call it The Royalty.) The first was if you were downstairs never to sit in the front rows, and the second was never to sit anywhere near a gangway in any part of the building. To sit near the first location would mean sustaining a constant bombardment of apple cores, orange peel and nut shells from the *bourgeoisie* sitting up in the gallery (admission one penny extra). To sit near the second would ensure great gales of disinfectant billowing around you as Arthur, the belligerent and shortsighted attendant, sprayed everything he could see with a huge old Flit-gun.

Value for money at The Trinity was excellent. You saw a film, usually a Tom Mix cowboy or perhaps a comedy, a cartoon feature, a three-month-old newsreel and, of course, the never-ending serial. It was mainly the serials that we all came for, *Flash Gordon* being arguably the favourite. A really determined young film-goer could even spend a Saturday afternoon there at no extra cost by the simple subterfuge of visiting the toilet at the end of the serial and waiting there until the afternoon showing. I confess I used this ruse only once: not even equipped with sewer boots and a mask would I have attempted it again.

The outrageous inflation that hit us when admission increased to threepence presented a financial problem. However there were all sorts of jobs that a boy might do for a little pocket money. Helping the 'cat's meat man', for example.

Every morning Ernie, a tall, slim young man, would pedal an ancient tricycle around the neighbouring streets. The trike consisted of a large wooden box and a well worn chopping block. This block was some six inches thick at each end but its centre sagged like a workhouse bed to a thickness of about an inch or so. A great side of horse-flesh lay in the bottom of the box, together with a pile of old newspapers. On each street corner, Ernie would stop and carve a fresh quantity of the meat, wrapping it into neat little rolled packages. Ernie would then be in the market for a boy to secure the packages underneath the door-knockers of customers. (This system was not entirely catproof. Tim, our own cat, had developed the trick of running straight up people's doors and stealing other cats' dinners.) As a source of income, Ernie was very much a last resort. His own wages were doubtless abysmal and he never paid any boy more than twopence for hours of running up and down stairs. The ride from street to street, sitting on his foul-smelling chopping block, was scant consolation. Apart from the fact that only one of us could be employed at a time, the gang needed something a little more rewarding than that.

We found it in the timber business, or, more accurately, firewood. A riverside saw-mill opened early on Saturday mornings and there half a sackful of wooden block could be bought for a penny. Around eight o'clock, each of the gang could be seen scurrying along Southwark Bridge Road with his sack slung purposefully over his shoulder. A convoy of kids would then part drag, part carry their loads back to Collinson Street and for the next hour sit industriously on the pavement, chopping the blocks into small kindling sticks. After this it was simply a matter of carrying armfuls of wood around Queen's Buildings, knocking on every door with the cry of 'Penny an armful!' Approximately six to eight armfuls could be conjured out of the contents of each sack. (We always picked the boy with the smallest arms to carry the kindling sticks.) With no overheads except for the sacks, and the chopper that we borrowed from my grandfather, we usually made at least 500 per cent profit.

As the children reached their teens and began to start work, so their membership of the small street gangs lessened. The teenagers who did stay fell mainly into two groups. The first, and easily the larger, consisted mainly of the sadder and more backward children, who still needed somewhere to belong. Usually known as 'Kings of the

Kids', they would try to use their few years' advantage over their increasingly rebellious juniors. Their reign lasted until some sort of showdown in which they lost face badly, when they would quietly fade from the scene. The second group also quietly faded eventually, but for rather different reasons. Its members formed the small hard-core who graduated to the senior gangs of the area: the Elephant and Castle gang, the Bricklayer's Arms gang and the Blackfriars gang. Many of these characters could be seen after a few months sporting razor-blades three-quarters hidden in the peak of their caps. Knuckle-dusters would bulge in their pockets and thin pencil-line moustaches would break out like impetigo on their top lip. We never really knew for sure if they were big-gang members or not. Very often they weren't. But it was a grand act, with everyone playing their parts very well.

I still had some five years to go before my decision was made. Yet I was beginning to realize that the big gangs were just not for me. I had studied their members from every angle and they had occasionally impressed my childish mind. Yes, I probably would have carried their razors – but I would not have been seen dead in their caps!

5. Oswald Mosley and me

If Saturdays were for commerce and the cinema, then Sundays were for socializing. While my mother's family lived opposite our flat in Queen's Buildings, my father's family lived in Hankey Place, a squiggly L-shaped street some three-quarters of a mile away, just over the border into Bermondsey. A half-hour Sunday afternoon stroll to the senior Cole household could occasionally net a penny from each of them. Dad had been one of ten children, five of whom were still at home. A good Sunday could therefore be worth as much as sevenpence. The only drawback to this generosity was that most of these donors were my aunts. Aunts were notoriously bad news for seven-year-old boys. Whenever they gave you a penny, they would always – but always – ruin the whole effect by also giving you a kiss. A lad could rub the wretched kiss off just as quickly and vigorously as he liked but, sure enough, next week another great wet plonker would be squelched on to his resentful face. Absolutely nothing would put them off. Socks around my ankles, candles from my nose, arse out of my trousers – all to no avail. They would grab me as if I were a grimy Clark Gable – and squelch!

It was during one of these ingratiating visits to Hankey Place that I received my baptism into large-scale violence. The route from Queen's Buildings to Hankey Place was via Long Lane in Bermondsey, a long, narrow, cobbled road that served as a cut-through to the docks. During the week it was full of slow-moving, rumbling, bumper-to-bumper traffic. Numerous haulage firms and carters' warehouses were scattered along its entire length, with small nests of shops grouped at intervals between these firms. The very first group consisted of a cat's meat shop, a chemist's, The Working Men's Dining Rooms and Henry Trappitt's, Greengrocer. In addition to the usual vegetables, Henry Trappitt sold small bags of coal at highly inflated prices and hired out 'Costermonger's Barrows at Competitive Terms'. In contrast to this weekday confusion, Sundays were practically tranquil. Scarcely a vehicle was to be seen. No one in the vicinity owned a car and all lorries and carts were garaged out of sight. The lane, therefore, was usually quite empty on Sundays, with just a handful of customers gathered at Trappitt's and a few more at the cat's meat shop.

One mild October Sunday, I meandered out of the Borough High Street and made to turn into Long Lane. It was my habit to push 'button B' of every telephone box that I passed, just in case someone had forgotten to reclaim their twopence. It was also worthwhile inserting one's finger up the cash chute. Sometimes, far more un-scrupulous children might have stuffed it with newspaper. If this was indeed the case, this timely removal of the blockage could result in numerous pennies cascading out all over the floor of the callbox. Unfortunately, on this particular trip a solitary policeman stood in the doorway of each kiosk, like a sentry in a box. The police, it would seem, had suddenly become determined to stamp out this occasionally fruitful exercise. (I only many years later discovered the real reason for this lone occupation: in those days before police radios, the telephone was their only means of communication.) Feeling somewhat cheated, I sauntered on. Like most small boys, I walked with my head down. A sudden roar caused me to look quickly up. There, barely twenty yards in front, were more people than I had ever seen before in my lifetime. Many of them were singing and chanting and carrying banners. Dozens of policemen were in cordons across the road.

'Where do you think you're going to, sonny?' asked one of them, not unkindly.

'Goin' to see me gran, o' course,' I replied, quite surprised that anyone, least of all a copper, should really be interested in my destination.

'Where does your gran live?'

'In 'Ankey Place.'

'Well, I'm sorry, but you won't be able to see her today. Long Lane and Hankey Place are quite dangerous at the moment, so you'll have to go back home. Go on, off you go.' He turned me around and pointed me back whence I came.

This retreat was never really on. My curiosity would never have allowed it. I quickly doubled down a side alley and through the courtyard of a tenement block. Within a couple of minutes, I was fifty yards behind the police cordon and well into Long Lane. The lane was truly an amazing sight. Two great barriers were strewn across the road. The first consisted of Henry Trappitt's costermonger's barrows rammed into each other and piled high from wall to wall. The second barrier, further along the road, consisted mainly of a huge old boiler that had been manhandled from Harpic's factory in Hankey Place. Both barriers were completely blocking the roadway and there was no way that I could pass. So I made another detour and soon arrived at gran's house in Hankey Place.

All of the family was in a state of excitement and they practically leapt on me as I walked down the street. 'What're you doing here?' seemed to be the favourite

question. First the copper and now gran! I was beginning
to feel really important.

'I've come to see you all,' I lied. Somehow it did not seem
ethical to admit that I only came for the money.

'Does your mother know where you are?'

'Yeh,' I replied unconvincingly, suddenly remembering
that mum had forbidden me to go anywhere near the place.
'She said it was all right. What's goin' on, gran?' I asked,
quickly trying to change the subject.

'It's Mosley. He's going to march down Long Lane and
there's a big crowd trying to stop him!'

'Are *we* goin' to stop him, gran?' I had absolutely no idea
who Mosley was but it sounded like it might just be fun.

'No, we're all goin' up to your Auntie Lil's balcony and
we're going to watch.'

'Mosley-watching' was a Bermondsey pastime that day.
Thousands of people had arrived in Long Lane from all
over the country and the locals treated it as an interesting
Sunday diversion. Not until many years later did I discover
the real significance of that day. Sir Oswald Mosley and his
black-shirted fascist party had originally planned a march
through the East End of London but the Home Secretary
had banned it because so many Jewish people lived there.
Sir Oswald then changed his route to one that ran parallel,
but this time on the south side of the river. The fact that
the route was changed made no difference to the
protestors. As far as they were concerned, Mosley was
Mosley wherever he marched. They would as happily fight
him in Long Lane as they would in the Mile End Road.
Mosley did not mind either. His routes were always
planned for the maximum publicity. A confrontation
would achieve that publicity equally well, whether it were
north or south of the river. Even the locals were not too
distressed. After all, they could watch the ensuing battle

with interest and perhaps even take part. It would not be fair to assume from this that everyone was in favour of the march. They were not. Some local people strongly objected. Henry Trappitt for one.

Aunt Lil's balcony was on the fourth floor and neatly overlooked the first of the barricades. I watched with interest as some of the demonstrators uprooted a young tree, pushed it into the pile of costermonger's barrows and attached a red flag to it. At this, several of them began to sing loudly. I was pleasantly surprised to realize that it was a tune I knew quite well. However, I noticed their words were quite different to the lyric that I had been taught. Their words rang out:

> The people's flag is deepest red,
> It shrouded oft our martyred dead.

Yet the words that all the kids in our street would daringly sing were:

> The working class can kiss my arse,
> I've got the foreman's job at last.

I was very tempted to join in with my own version but I just had the feeling that it might not quite be gran's style.

Suddenly a great argument took place between the demonstrators and several of Aunt Lil's neighbours. It seemed that strong objections had been raised to the uprooting of the tree. Heaven knows, trees were short enough in Bermondsey as it was. Verbal abuse began to pour from the flats on to the singing protestors. This dissension soon ceased, however, when the police began to advance on the barricade. At last! This was what everyone had stayed at home for!

Oswald Mosley and me

The first advance was met by a hail of missiles and the broken blue ranks quickly retreated. Their second advance was much more determined but still pieces of masonry continued to pelt into their midst. Again they retreated. 'Look, they've got their truncheons out now!' ran the message through the watchers. Sure enough, the line of charging coppers crashed into the barricade and many violent skirmishes took place. Some policemen began to disperse the barrows, while others laid about themselves with their truncheons. A few defenders retreated to the next barrier but most either sat down to nurse their wounds or assembled into small vociferous groups.

The line of policemen moved on to this next barrier but the resistance they met was spasmodic and half-hearted. Casualties with bleeding heads and arms sat around everywhere, police and demonstrators alike. Because of the many street obstructions, ambulances could not get through. The injured therefore just sat in doorways and on the kerbsides and waited. There was a sudden burst of activity as a group of demonstrators pushed a car towards the rear of the police who were still dismantling the barricade. This appeared to be no more than a token gesture, as the car failed to travel in a straight line. Instead it rolled threateningly towards a group of injured sitting by the roadside. By the simple process of moving on to the pavement, the casualties were able to ensure their own safety. The slow momentum of the car was easily halted by the kerbstones.

There now appeared to be no set pattern to the activities. Groups of arguing and fighting people were scattered all around the neighbouring streets.

'Hey, young man! It's about time you went home – it'll be dark soon,' instructed Aunt Lil.

Twenty minutes later, I picked my way through the

debris of Long Lane. On the credit side I had seen some great fights, had a piece of Aunt Lil's cake and collected sixpence. On the debit side, I was certain to receive a wallop when my mother found out where I had been, I had gleaned not a penny from the telephone boxes and I had sustained four wet kisses from aunts. On balance I had just about won – but it had been a damn close thing.

6. A right little street-raker

By the time I reached my eighth summer, I had become, in the words of my grandmother, 'a right little street-raker'.

With such a maze of streets, lanes and alleys, all within a mile radius of home, there seemed to be a new exploration to be made every day. Yet in spite of all of these discoveries and adventures, the one amenity that Southwark really lacked (and still does) was a park. During school holidays, we kids would make determined attempts to find one. Small groups of us would trek, safari-like, from the wilds of Waterloo to the alleys and wharves of Dockhead. The absence of a park was quite bearable during the foggy winter months, but the long summer days screamed for open space and grass.

There were, in fact, two small open spaces that had finally to satisfy our needs. One was the rather grandly named Newington Gardens Recreation Ground, a small grassless space at the rear of the Inner London Sessions. Its swings and slides were built on the site of the old Horsemonger Lane Gaol, hence the more local name of 'Gaol Park'. This site had been a favourite spot for public executions some eighty years earlier. We kids felt really deprived that we had missed them. Other than these few swings and a sandpit, Gaol Park had little to offer an adventurous young chap.

Our other mecca of entertainment was yet another grandly named enclosure – Geraldine Mary Harmsworth

Park, known to all as 'Bedlam' because it covered the site of the old lunatic asylum, where lords and their ladies ambled each Sunday while being amused by the inmates. Two small recreation parks, one a former gallows and the other an asylum, somehow explains a great deal about north Southwark. Bedlam Park was excruciatingly boring: a square, flat open space, with nothing at all to fire the imagination of an honest street-urchin. It is true that this park housed the superbly equipped Imperial War Museum, but our attempts to enter the building were always repulsed by the porters, who showed the tenacity of Wellington's guards. 'Thou shalt not pass,' was their order of the day. This, translated into War Museum English, became, 'Oy, you! Out!' They delivered that line so regularly and so well that I was fourteen years old before I discovered that people were actually allowed to enter museums at all.

During my eighth year, however, a development took place at Bedlam that revolutionized our school summer holidays. A children's open-air swimming pool was completed, alongside the museum. This pool seemed as large as the Pacific. In reality it measured ninety feet by eighty feet with a maximum depth of three feet. So many children flocked to the pool that sometimes one had difficulty seeing the surface. Most of the boys splashed around in just their underpants while the girls wore their vests and knickers. For many kids it was the only day of the week when their bodies actually touched water. The constant smell of bleach and carbolic indicated that the authorities were aware of this fact.

Only young children were allowed into the pool, but grown-ups could sit on the nearby benches which were separated from the pool-side by a railing fence. Occasionally a mother would supervise her child from there, but on the whole these benches were frequented by middle-aged and elderly men who found the triple attractions of sunshine, half-naked kids and a female lifeguard irresistible. The lifeguard was a tall, slim girl who wore a white bathing-cap and a sombre black one-piece costume. Unfortunately for the viewing gallery, she also wore a ground-length white towelling robe. As she patrolled the perimeter, the occasional flash of knee might be revealed, but the only flesh of any significance was in the mind of the beholder.

This frustration finally bothered one watcher more than most. He leaned over the fence and called in general to our group. 'Wanna earn twopence each?' We were instantly all ears. All we had to do it seemed, was play a game. In this game, one of us had to duck down into the water and the rest of us had to shout 'Help'.

'What then?' asked Rosie Pilbeam suspiciously.

'That's it, that's all you've got to do,' explained the man. 'I'll give each of you twopence then. That's fair enough, ain't it?'

I thought it was just about the fairest thing I had ever heard in my life. Rosie, however, was distrustful.

'Give us the twopence first, then,' she demanded.

'Nah, look,' said the man, slowly emphasizing every word, 'I just wanna play a game on the lifeguard, that's all. When she comes around to this side of the pool, one of you 'as to jump in an' pretend that they're drowning. After that you gets your money, all right?'

While explaining the routine to us, he had taken a handful of pennies from his trouser pocket and was slowly counting them. Each of the boys thought it was just about the easiest thing he had ever heard, and we were worried that our benefactor might change his mind. Rosie, however, would not let go.

'Give us the money first,' she repeated.

If this went on, I could see her ruining the whole financial project. I decided to interrupt.

'Charlie can do it,' I blurted out quickly. ''E'll jump in, won't you, Charlie?'

'No, I won't!' protested the gutless Charlie. 'I can't swim. You jump in yourself,' he added vindictively.

'I can't swim either!' I whined.

What the situation now needed was a good swimming volunteer. The whole group, with Charlie and I setting the pace, now stared intently at our best swimmer – Rosie Pilbeam.

Rosie said nothing to us but turned once more to the man. ''Ere, you're not one o' them dirty old sods that me mum told me to watch out for, are you? You don't want me to take off me drawers before I jump in, do you?'

I was absolutely flabbergasted at this suggestion. Why on earth should anyone pay each of us twopence if Rosie took off her drawers? I had seen Rosie dozens of times without them – any time that she wanted a wee, she simply squatted over the nearest drainhole – and in my opinion Rosie Pilbeam's bum was not worth a single penny of anyone's money.

'Look!' snapped the man, now obviously losing patience. 'The lifeguard's around this side o' the pool. D'you want twopence each or don't you? I don't mind, it's all the same to me. If you don't want it, you can go without.' So saying, he slid the money back into his pocket.

This impending loss was all too much for Charlie Martin. With a solitary great heave, he thrust the questioning Rosie into three feet of sun-kissed, diluted carbolic. Yet as quick as he was, Rosie still managed to emit two 'F's and a 'B' before she hit the water. I looked at Charlie with a newfound admiration. That's courage, that is, I thought. Rosie'll kill him when she gets out!

"Elp, 'elp,' chorused the enterprising Charlie. 'Rosie's fallen in the deep end!'

Realizing that the damage was now well and truly done, the rest of us joined in. "Elp, 'elp!' we echoed.

It worked like a charm. The lifeguard looked up quickly then slipped out of her robe, all in one movement. She ran forward for a few yards, then leapt smoothly into space to land with a splash alongside the struggling Rosie, who was now sitting on the bottom. The dull black costume changed instantly into wet sparkling life as its wearer reached down into the shallows. Presto! She pulled out her arm and the spluttering Rosie broke the surface. I was suddenly aware of a bewildering confusion. I liked Rosie quite a lot, she was possibly my best mate. Yet even at this early age, still some years away from that first tingle in my loins, I wondered why that lifeguard in her shiny black costume should look so much better than our Rosie in her wet vest. Was that why we were to get twopence each?

'Charlie Martin, I'm gonna fuckin' kill you!'

I remember wondering which of us would get Charlie's cut if she did. Charlie decided the question was purely academic and therefore did not require his presence at its conclusion. He was over the fence and halfway out of the park before Rosie got her second breath.

The lifeguard perched the cursing victim on the edge of the pool then swung herself up and out of the water. As the dripping pair stood at the poolside, I turned quickly to our new friend in order to claim our hard-earned twopence. I was mildly surprised to see that he was leaning back, with his trousers unbuttoned and his willie in his hand. I recognized the pose instantly. It was the same one that the boys at school adopted, when we tried to see who could wee up the wall the highest. I found that the whole situation was becoming more confusing by the minute.

'Cor, look! I told yer!' yelled the panting Rosie. ''E *is* a dirty old sod! 'E's got 'is dickie out!'

Our potential benefactor then gave a quick sigh. Spinning round on his toes, he followed the same route taken seconds earlier by the fleeing Charlie.

Now obviously none of us was actually pleased by these developments, but Rosie was positively demented. She was so furious that she had great difficulty focusing her wrath on one particular target. She lashed out in all directions. Charlie, of course, came in for the lion's share of her tongue. I soon recovered from my own disappointment at this incident. I did, however, make a mental note to pay closer attention next time that Rosie strained on a drain. After all, there was always the possibility that it could be worth twopence.

7. Hop-picking

'I've got me letter! I've got it!'

The annual midsummer cry would be heard floating from window to window, throughout the length and breadth of Queen's Buildings. Immediately fear would begin to grip those who had yet to receive their 'letter'. This letter was simply a reply to an application that would have been made several weeks earlier, in the spring. At that time, the neatest writer in the family would have written to a farmer in Kent applying for a season's hop-picking. ''Opping', as the project was always called, was as important to pre-war Londoners as buffaloes were to the Indians. It meant money, holidays, fresh air, grass and animals. The four to six weeks spent in the fields would be a complete change from every other day of the year.

The hop-fields were in an area that stretched from the North Downs across the Weald of Kent, from Tonbridge to Canterbury. Here, 90 per cent of English hop-fields were to be found. Nowadays it is one hour's travelling time from south-east London, probably too near to be classified as a Sunday afternoon drive. Yet up until the 1940s it was a place where thousands of Londoners would spend at least a month of every year: not just families, sometimes whole streets moved out, like latter-day Israelites. They would troop off to a corner of Kent to find the promised land, a land that would be flowing with milk stout and honey.

Hop-picking had one unbeatable attraction for us

children. It began on the first week of the autumn term. Therefore, instead of returning to the lovely Miss Jones on the first week in September, we would not arrive back until early October.

Most families travelled down to Kent on the 'Hopper's Special', a special-rate train that left London Bridge Station in the early hours of the morning and also conveyed the milk and newspapers. All provisions required on the long stay in Kent would be placed in the "Opping Box', which was usually a large tea-chest, or possibly an old trunk, but often it was nothing more than a series of stout heavy planks, nailed together in box form. Whatever its final shape, it would need wheels: the weight it was to bear would be enormous. For eleven months of the year, the box would sit in a backyard or on a balcony, doubling as a coal-container. Now, for the next few weeks, it would be a table. A couple of days before the journey, therefore, it would be scrubbed spotless and its wheels oiled and cleaned. Absolutely everything had to be crammed into these boxes. Many families even took wallpaper and drawing pins. Special iron pots were also needed. These utensils would spend most of the next few weeks in the heart of a large wood-fire. A huge iron saucepan, rather like a witch's cauldron, would be used for every form of cooking. This, the treasured 'opping pot, would be an absolute heirloom to most families. All manner of dishes were prepared in that pot. My mother could even manage a roast!

There was one definite advantage in having a coalman in the family. We did not have to join the undignified scramble for the 'Hopper's Special'. Uncle's old horse Prince had sadly died, but he was now in possession of an equally old coal-lorry. A bucketful of soapy water and a stiff broom can completely renovate such a vehicle. Unfortunately, not everyone could travel in the cabin of the lorry. Some of us therefore travelled on the open back, a thick tarpaulin keeping out most of the wind. The subsequent hours spent thawing out were but a small price to pay. Even though our journey was now door-to-door, our time of departure was no more civilized than that of our neighbours who were to travel by train, because Uncle Tim was required to return to London by dawn in order to load up at the coal wharf. I would bury myself in the thick coat of Old Joe and sleep soundly for most of the way.

The men in the family, of course, still had to go to work, but they would visit us at weekends. Only the women, the children and the unemployed males actually made the journey.

Each family was notified in their letter of the accommodation allocated to them. It consisted usually of (a) one corrugated-iron hut, creosoted on the outside, lime-washed on the inside, possibly with a wooden floor but usually an unevened soil; (b) the nearby stream, or, if lucky, a well; (c) a tiny communal hut, some forty yards away from our living quarters and built over an almost bottomless pit – the lavatory. Straw was provided for bedding and a daily supply of long sticks (always called faggots) was allocated for heating and cooking. The cooking was of course carried out over the open camp-fire.

Most of the hut would be taken up with the huge bed. Its great size was essential because everyone had to sleep in it. Our own party would consist of mum, gran, two aunts, one cousin, my baby brother and myself. If the bed was crowded during the week, it was like the black hole at weekends when the men arrived! The huts were clustered in groups of about ten or a dozen, with privacy and space non-existent. Should anyone as much as turn over, straw-filled mattresses would announce the movement to

67

sleepers three huts away. If turning over in bed was noisy, then a trip to the lavatory was deafening. As for any weekend hanky-panky, well, half of Kent could have bought tickets. I did daringly ask my mother in latter years how young newly weds tackled this problem. After all, a four- to six-week separation with just a crowded occasional weekend meeting could be quite frustrating, to say the least. 'Well, there were always the sacks of hops,' she replied wistfully, 'though they did stick in your bum,' she added, as a painful afterthought.

Each hut member had a task to perform at breakfast. The children's job was to draw water for the early morning tea, and we invariably got more water in our wellington boots than we did in our bucket. Every September I would experience four weeks of trench-foot.

After breakfast and the skimpiest of washes, I would trail behind the adults up to the hop-field. There the farm foreman would allocate each family a wood-and-canvas bin about six feet in length, two or three feet wide and almost waist-high. It was carried along by means of two poles slotted through it, rather like stretcher handles. The hops were clustered on the vines that trailed down some twelve feet from overhead wires. The vines would be tugged down by a farmhand with a long pole. He would never be the brightest of individuals and would answer to the predictable name of 'pole-puller'. Once he had pulled down several yards of vine, each family would immediately gather round their bin and start to pick furiously. Soon the cry would echo up and down the rows, 'Pole-puller!' Woe betide that gentleman if he did not respond at once. For four weeks he lived in total dread of my grandmother.

As the bin began to fill, so gran would appoint herself 'fluffer-upper'. This was an extremely important task. The farmer paid for his hops by the bushel. A good fluffer-upper could manage an extra bushel from each bin-load. Once the bin was full, the foreman would arrive with a basket that measured exactly a bushel. He would then scoop hops into a large sack. Heaven help the scooper who filled his basket too high. It was amazing how two people could have such contrasting ideas as to what constituted a level basketful. The rate for the job was about a shilling for three bushels. A large family of good pickers could manage around forty bushels in a day. As the bin was emptied, the quantity would be registered and payment would be made on the last day of picking.

The duration of a child's picking was about ten minutes. The novelty of the work soon paled and we would then go off to explore this whole new world. Although many farmers must have been sorely tempted, they never actually shot a child. It was indeed a tremendous life. Other than being tossed by a bull, falling in the River Medway, or contracting galloping foot-rot, we were quite safe. We would only venture back to the hop fields when we were hungry, usually about every hour. We did, in fact, suffer greatly from this endless hunger. 'It's this fresh air,' gran would say. 'They're not used to it.' None would dispute her.

From time to time salesmen would call at the hop-fields. Bakers with large cane baskets carried an assortment of wares, all smelling superbly: Chelsea buns, Tottenham cake, burnt rolls and crusty loaves. All were baked to torment the sensitive nostrils of a starving lad. These rather wholesome goodies would often be preceded by a commodity that looked far from nourishing. A thin, swarthy individual in a dirty turban would enter the field, vigorously ringing a large cracked handbell. A filthy tin box would be strung from a cord around his neck. This container was approximately the size of two biscuit tins.

His strange falsetto cry penetrated every corner of the field: 'In-di-ian tof-fee-ee. In-di-n tof-fee-ee.' Speaking purely as a boy who would eat just about anything, even I was repelled by Indian toffee. I now suspect the ingredients had been no nearer India than a back alley in Chatham. On the one occasion that I ventured to try it, I found it vaguely reminiscent of sweet shredded horse-dung. Be that as it may, there were still customers for it. When in later years I read that the life-expectancy in Calcutta was about twenty-five years, I thought that someone should have taken a good look at their toffee.

These wares drew not only hungry and inquisitive children, but thousands of hungry and inquisitive wasps. These fearless, persistent creatures were a totally new hazard to us kids.

Flies we were used to. They would swarm in the open windows in Queen's Buildings, as even they sought sanctuary from the over-ripe rubbish chutes. But wasps were totally different. They fought back! When half a dozen settled on your Chelsea bun, the best line of defence was to drop it and scream. After all, it could always be picked up again once they had left. Wasps on a bun was second only to earwigs in a bed on the list of hop-picking terrors.

There were always one or two gypsy encampments nearby. They would wander up and down the hop-rows, selling sprigs of heather and clothes-pegs, while telling fortunes to the gullible. Many hop-pickers went in total awe of them. 'If you don't be'ave yourself,' some children would be told, 'I'll sell you to the gypsies for clothes-pegs!'

I had great difficulty understanding this betrayal. After all, if you had sold your son and heir to a gypsy, why on earth should you buy him back as a clothes-peg?

As the late afternoon fell, the children would gravitate

back to the huts. Wooden faggots would be gathered and more water would certainly be needed. There were times when I wondered what grown-ups did with all this water. I seemed to spend the whole of September pouring it either in or out of my boots. As the last of the pickers trooped wearily back from the fields, so the dying sun would hand over to the newly born camp-fires. The chill, dew-laden air would coax us ever closer to the crackling flames. Everywhere was the smell of food. That mug of strong smoky tea was a meal in itself. It was the best time of day.

When the meal had been eaten and the plates washed (another bloody trip with the bucket), we would usually be joined by other families. As we sat shoulder to shoulder around the fire, some would see pictures in its embers. I don't think I have ever sat around a camp-fire without at least one visionary seeing these pictures. I would stare vainly at the glow until my lashes singed and my eye-balls melted – but all I saw was hot ashes. They would flicker and dance, fade and rekindle, hiss and crackle, but they were always just hot ashes, nothing more.

'Come on, you kids, bedtime!' would come the first call. The cry would then be taken up all around the camp-fires. 'Bedtime, kids!' 'Come on, you lot, 'op it!' 'No arguing – bed!' No matter how I peered, I could never discover which fireside first started the rot. They would just be faceless voices from the dark. Soon, of course, I would recognize a voice.

'Come on, Harry, bedtime,' would come mum's authoritative cry. A token wash (in order to save water), then a quick climb on to that huge bed. The first one to bed usually lay in the middle and the subsequent sleepers built slowly outwards. The cold damp straw penetrated both sheet and mattress cover and I would screw myself up tightly, just to keep warm. Soon, though, another six sleeping bodies would lie either side of me. Cold would not be a problem then.

Hop-picking ceased at one o'clock on Saturday, providing the opportunity for some shopping at nearby Wateringbury village. In preparation for our influx of visitors, a huge meat-pudding would be placed in the hopping-pot. An equally large spotted-dick would follow it. The train that puffed its way into distant Wateringbury station could clearly be seen from our huts. Ample warning was therefore given of the arrival of the weekenders. I would be sent out to scout as they climbed the hill towards us. 'See if granddad is with them!' There was nothing that could be done even if he was. But it at least gave everyone two minutes longer to prepare.

After a huge meal and a swopping of news, all of the adults adjourned in the evening to the pub. Unfortunately, not every public house welcomed hop-pickers. Our gathering of huts, plus their guests, would need to troop some two or three miles to another village. Even here their presence was barely tolerated. The landlord would probably have installed a 'Special Hopper's Bar' for the duration of the season. No self-respecting licensee would allow any of the hop-pickers to use his saloon, or even his public bar. An outhouse was usually set aside, with barrels of beer and saw-dust on the floor. Hence the rather grandly named 'Special Hopper's Bar'. The children were left behind, in charge of the huts, fires and any domestic animals that may have been brought along.

'. . . And don't let the fire go out!' would have been the most important final instruction.

Crossing the strange dark countryside to go to a pub was not an easy task. If it was difficult to go, how much more difficult it was then to return. Difficult for everyone, that is, except granddad. He would somehow always become separated from the main body of drinkers. Whether this was just a series of coincidences, or a deliberate attempt to avoid him, I never discovered. But I know where my suspicions lay. The old man had many gifts, his capacity for drink being among his greatest. He did, however, have another gift which in its way was even more astonishing. He possessed a homing instinct that was unsurpassed, even by pigeons. No matter where, or how drunk he was, no matter what the weather or temperature, he could always find his way home. Half an hour after the rest of the family had left the bright lights of the Special Hopper's Bar, he would emerge melodiously. For one minute he would pause to adjust his dim eyes to the complete darkness. Then, resuming his song, he would toddle off into the strange total blackness of a hop-field night. Streams and stiles, paths and puddles, hedges and ditches, he would negotiate them all to the faggot-fire that burned so brightly, some three miles away. It was a feat that would daunt a platoon of nocturnal infantry, yet he did it every time with unfailing accuracy.

In twos and threes the family would return to the camp, like bees to the hive. Eventually everyone except the old man would assemble around the fire. Faintly in the distant darkness, we would hear the last two lines of a familiar song.

> Nah there ain't a lady livin' in the land
> as I'd swop fer me dear old dutch.

Granddad was returning home in romantic mood.

My father, who was a great tea-drinker, would busy himself with the huge black kettle. Large steaming mugs would then be passed around and granddad would lead the singing. Jokes and stories would be told and reminiscences relived.

With the dawn barely three hours away, last quick visits to the bottomless pit would be made. One by one we would slide rustlingly into the noisy straw bed, there to lie stiff and still like tin soldiers in a box.

Within a very short time, strange birds would be singing, and somewhere a distant cock would crow. The first of the early morning risers would edge from between the line of sleeping bodies and take the wet stroll to the bottomless pit. I say 'wet' because every hopping morning that I remember started with a thick white mist, hopefully to be followed by a bright sunny day. Even today, after all these years, I still classify a misty start as a 'typical hopping morning'.

Slowly the whole enclave of huts would wake. I always viewed weekends with mixed feelings. While it was nice to see different faces, there was always far more water to fetch on a Sunday. On balance, though, that chore was more than offset by the Sunday smell of fried bacon. After a leisurely breakfast, the menfolk would prepare for the long walk to the Special Hopper's Bar, returning as if by magic only seconds before the two o'clock dinner.

While the grown-ups spent the afternoon relaxing around the fire, the kids would go scrumping. Everyone who had visited the hop-fields would be expected to return home with at least a bag of apples. It was down to us to provide them.

Soon everyone would trail down to Wateringbury station, to see off the weekenders. The dark-green steam-engine would gradually appear in the distance, puffing great rolling clouds of white smoke. These clouds would at first roll quickly down to the Medway; then, having arrived, they seemed so taken by the river that they would stop, remaining poised quite still just above the water, as if in admiration.

In all of my childhood, I never once saw a cloud cross the Medway.

Sunday evenings were something of an anticlimax. There would, of course, be more water to draw, but then an early night would be ordered. Most kids made a token protest, but secretly we were pleased to climb into a bed that offered more room than just our own body space.

For year after year, generation after generation, nothing much happened to change the way of life at the hop-fields. Then, finally, came the war. Nothing was to be the same again. Bombers and fighters; Messerschmitts and Spitfires; shells and bullets; all ingratiated themselves over that small corner of Kent.

My mother had first taken me hop-picking when I was six weeks old. She took my brother when he was six days old! Yet even she could not tackle a war there. After that last peaceful autumn, we never returned to the fields again. The war had smashed the continuity, and mechanization became the order of the day. A machine did not go scrumping, nor need a Special Hopper's Bar.

A few months ago, while returning home from the coast, I decided to make a detour and call in at the old site. Gone were the huts, there was not a sign of the faggots. Even the little shop that sold everything from boiled sweets to boiled ham had vanished. There was no bottomless pit and I could not find the stream. I never saw as much as a single hop.

It's true that Wateringbury station is still there, although it is now serviced by boring little electric trains. But the Medway! What has happened to the Medway? In my childhood it was as wide as the Mississippi, yet now it is little more than a brook. Thank heaven that the hills are still there. They may not be as steep as they were, but they still stretch away to that distant hospitable village. And

Policeman's Prelude

how about granddad? Does his ghost walk those hills as he
returns singing from some sky-based Special Hopper's
Bar? If it does, I bet that he is terrifying the gypsies. He
would have enjoyed that, the wicked old sod.

8. War! Or Winkleshells?

As a nine-year-old child whose interest lay mainly in the street and the Saturday morning cinema, I was fairly immune to world politics. It had, however, already filtered down even to me that something very unusual was brewing. People kept talking about a 'crisis' and a war. Whatever a 'crisis' was, it certainly made for a direct opening topic, every time that two grown-ups conversed.

'I don't think there'll be one, Gladys, do you? My Bert says they wouldn't dare. He says we beat 'em last time and we'd do it again.'

'That's what my Fred says too, Maude. He reckons we've got a secret dark-ray that no one can beat.'

Well, Fred and Bert may have thought that we had it all sewn up, but this confidence did not seem to permeate down to Charles Dickens School. There Miss Atkins assembled us in the hall and gave each of us a slip of paper explaining what would be expected of us if a war was to break out. The first thing they wanted us to do was to leave London. We were to take Miss Atkins's notes home to our parents without fail. The whole school was to go away somewhere in the country. Most of the children eagerly looked forward to this trip. We thought it would be something like hop-picking.

That evening, my parents decided to discuss with me the possibility of leaving London, which made me feel extremely grown-up. I discovered that wherever the school was to be sent, it was certainly not to the hop-fields. But if the school closed and I was not evacuated, there would be no school for me to attend. This fact appealed to me greatly, and I was pleased when mum concluded, 'I think that we should stay in London.'

'I ain't goin' away!' blurted Rosie the next morning, before I had a chance to tell her of my important discussion.

'Why's that, Rosie?' I asked.

'Me mum says that if you're evacuated, you could go to all sorts of funny 'ouses. Me mum says that they might not be very clean ones.'

I glanced quickly at Charlie who was walking with us to school. The only place that I could think of less clean than Rosie's home was the council tip.

Charlie shrugged. 'We ain't goin' either,' he announced rather sadly.

'Why's that, Charlie?' asked Rosie.

'I 'as to go to 'ospital a lot, on account of me – well, on account of me being – ' he dropped his voice to a whisper – 'fat an' that.' He paused for a moment and then continued in a more normal tone. 'My dad says that they don't 'ave proper 'ospitals in the country. 'E reckons they only 'ave vets. 'E thinks we'll be all better off 'ere.'

'So we're all staying, then?' I asked, brightening considerably.

'Looks like it!' beamed Rosie.

Charlie dropped his gaze and said nothing.

In the event of a war breaking out, we were listed as the only three children not to be evacuated from Miss Jones's class. There were, in fact, barely a dozen abstentions throughout the whole school.

It was soon summer holiday time and the potential war, evacuation and vets were all forgotten. We spent almost

every day in the open-air swimming pool. There were, however, changes taking place all around us. Everywhere basements were being reinforced, sandbags filled and trenches
dug. Hexagonal-shaped concrete huts with slit openings
appeared at many junctions almost overnight. I was never
really sure of their function. Some kids said they were
machine-gun nests, but other kids used them as lavatories.

On the last Friday of our school summer holiday, I
awoke to massive confusion. The radio and the newspapers
were full of instructions for those who were to leave
London. Children seemed to be everywhere with their
satchels, gas-masks and labels. I suddenly felt quite left out
of it. Charlie, Rosie and I ran down to the school to wave
goodbye to our classmates. Outside the gates was a line of
double-decker buses. The whole school sang, cheered and
waved to anyone who passed by. The teachers looked
totally harassed but the kids, except for the odd sniveller,
appeared to be loving every minute of it. It looked for all
the world like one huge school outing.

As the last of the buses throbbed away, the world
seemed strangely empty and quiet.

'I wish I'd gone now,' murmured Rosie wistfully, as she
crouched over a drainhole with her knickers around her
ankles.

'So do I,' I responded.

Charlie quietly cried. 'It's all right for you,' he blubbed.
'You didn't wanna go – but I did.'

We walked back to Queen's Buildings with an air of
dejection. It was a new experience to each of us.

'I think I'm gonna go indoors an' draw pictures of all the
kids goin' away,' sniffed Charlie. 'I'll see you later.' Charlie
was beginning to do this more and more often: as he
became fatter, so his desire to draw everything seemed to
increase. Strangely enough, he rarely drew anything much

at school. Yet the walls of the kitchen in which he slept were covered with the most startling real-life sketches.

'You know what this is like?' asked Rosie suddenly.

I shook my head. 'Nah, Rose, what's it like?'

'It's like that story that Miss Jones told us about the Pied Piper. All of the kids 'ave gone away an' there's only just us 'ere. I think it's a bit spooky really.'

I looked all around and she was right: not another child was to be seen. There were supposed to be two days to go but it seemed that we were already at war. I looked anxiously up at the sky but there were no bombers in sight, just a few broken clouds and smoke from the brewery opposite.

Events had not unfolded quite as Rosie and I had anticipated they would. We thought a war would be fun but it was becoming more like an inconvenience. There were few enough kids left to play with as it was, so Charlie's decision to shut himself away for the duration did not help at all.

'I don't think that I want a war now, Rose, d'you?' I asked regretfully.

'Well,' she began uncertainly, 'I wouldn't mind if it was a *short* one, p'raps all the kids would come back then.'

The next forty-eight hours were a real bore. The Saturday morning cinema had closed and so had the open-air swimming pool. In fact nowhere seemed to be open at all. The one bright spot was my firewood sales. The lack of competition meant that I had now cornered the market for the whole of Queen's Buildings. Yet even this palled. After I had made three shillings profit, I decided to quit.

Sunday dawned bright and clear. Dad said that we were all to listen to the radio at eleven o'clock. We would then discover if there really was to be a war. From 10.45 a.m. onwards, a stream of neighbours knocked at our door and scattered themselves around the living-room. These were people who had no radio and had arrived solely to hear the broadcast by Mr Chamberlain, the Prime Minister. They must also have been people who were really to be trusted, bearing in mind that our radio still ran illegally from the light socket! Fifteen people crouched apprehensively around our small brown bakelite set listening to the faltering tones: '. . . and I have to tell you that no such undertaking has been received. Therefore a state of war exists . . .'

There was just a few seconds' silence, as if it had all been rather too much for the assembly to absorb. Then a babble of conversation broke out, everyone talking at once. My mother disappeared momentarily into the front room and suddenly emerged with four gas-masks. The idea seemed to catch on, for everybody then scuttled back to their own flat in order to find their own masks. This gas-phobia lasted for all of a week. My mother insisted I took my mask everywhere I went, even to bed. A week later, however, while I was playing on a river barge, it fell into the Thames. I never saw it again.

No sooner had our neighbours left us than the sirens sounded to indicate that an air-raid was imminent. Everyone filed quietly down the staircase into the basement air-raid shelter, which consisted of just two reinforced rooms that smelt strongly of carbolic and cats. There were four of these rooms to each block entrance, and some seventy people to cater for – to say nothing of their pets. Dogs, cats, canaries and goldfish all barked, wriggled, chirruped and splashed.

Twenty minutes later the siren sounded again, this time to denote the 'all clear'. The raid had been a false alarm: the lone aircraft that had thrown London into its first experience of war was a French one. Suddenly, as we began to file back up the staircase, a sinister rat-tat-tat cut through the quiet Sunday air.

'Everybody down!' came the dramatic order from Albert Jenkins, the block's rather pompous air-raid warden. 'Machine guns!'

Everyone did go down and double-quick too. People thudded against those cold stone steps with their hands over their heads and their shoulders hunched. Suddenly a roar of laughter came from the forerunners, who had by now reached ground level. Not everyone, it transpired, had gone down to the shelter. Old Mrs Williamson had remained in her fifth-floor flat refusing to budge. Now that the 'all clear' had sounded, she had resumed her Sunday household tasks, one of these being the preparation of the Sunday menu. Like most Londoners, she would be having winkles for tea. The rat-tat-tat had been nothing more threatening than the old lady throwing her empty winkle shells down into the street! Albert Jenkins was never allowed to forget that.

We left the Queen's Buildings shelter never to return. Dad said we were in more danger from the shelter than ever we were from the bombs. Events were to prove him horrifically correct.

9. *Blitz*

As the weeks slipped unnoticeably by, so the first of the evacuees filtered home. By November, children were returning to London in droves. Every day another half dozen arrived back at Queen's Buildings. Some of the hair-raising tales they told of their treatment were beyond even our belief. Charlie, Rosie and I just had to grin and bear their wild stories. There was little we could offer in competition to their horrific tales.

The run-up to the end of 1939 was really a wild time for us kids. With no school to attend, the streets were ours. Many of the newly erected air-raid shelters were already falling into decay through sheer neglect. A dozen marauding youngsters can make a wonderful mess of a park dug-out trench.

By the new year, so many children had returned to London that some schools simply had to reopen. Although compulsory education had been suspended at the outbreak of war, pressure was now mounting to persuade children back into school. Teachers and school attendance officers wearing suitable arm-bands scoured the streets looking for renegade kids. It was extremely disconcerting to be playing on the river barges and hear a gruff adult voice cut across the water: 'Oy you! Why aren't you in school?' However, until the Education Act could be reinstated, attendance had to be voluntary. I eventually returned to Charles Dickens School for five half-days a week from late January onward. I personally did *not* volunteer. My mother, with hurtful alacrity, did so for me. By the spring of 1940 most of the schools, together with their pupils, were back to normal. The war was almost forgotten.

The fall of France in June brought about a renewed panic. Once again the schools were closed (though a form of schooling was to remain). Once again the masses left London. The adults all seemed to have a feeling of imminent catastrophe and, young as we were, we could also sense it. Sometimes we would climb the fourteen flights of stairs to the roof of Queen's Buildings and just stare south-eastwards. We were not even sure what we were looking for. We just knew that there, far beyond the silent barrier of the elephantine barrage-balloons, was *something*. This something was preparing itself – and it was preparing for us.

By the time the air-raids began along the south coast, the number of children left in London was equal to that of the first few days of the war. By the first week in August, all thoughts of school, both by ourselves and the authorities, were long abandoned. I had started to listen intently to the radio news broadcasts (a habit that has remained with me ever since). Sirens sounded daily and rumours were rife. There were distant explosions and vapour trails, but as yet, no Germans.

My father called a family meeting to decide what action we should take in the event of the now certain air-raids. Our one experience of the basement air-raid shelter had been enough for him to suggest an alternative. My Aunt Lylie and new baby cousin Stella had now moved into a second-floor flat in Queen's Buildings, further down the street. (My Uncle Tim had joined the air force.) Dad suggested, rather illogically, I thought, that we should be in less danger in Aunty's second-floor flat than we were in our own fourth-floor one. The result was that every time a siren sounded we hurried along to Aunt Lylie's. There we would be joined by my grandparents, my Aunt Liz and yet another baby-girl cousin, Renee. (Aunt Liz had been widowed since the early days of the war.)

To avoid the by now nightly disturbances, we finally began to sleep there. This presented a slight accommodation problem. There were then ten of us in a two-roomed flat. For some reason we all slept in the kitchen, the front room being, I presume, sacrosanct. My grandparents would sleep under the table while mum and dad slept on the floor. The rest of us lay top-to-toe in the big double bed that fitted neatly into a large recess.

Daily the gunfire came closer and so did the vapour trails. Soon they were overhead and the whistle of bombs and the rat-tat-tat of machine-guns became a way of life. It had taken almost a year but now Rosie Pilbeam, Charlie Martin and I were finally at war. If it was of any consolation to Hitler, we didn't like it one bit.

One of the most impressive aspects of the blitz was the way that people carried on with their normal lives. No matter how heavy the daylight raids, we rarely took shelter. Somehow Germans in the daylight did not seem anywhere near as sinister as Germans after dark. Dad still went to the factory, although for even longer hours, and mum still scrubbed the offices. Granddad went off with his pick and shovel and returned home just as drunk at the end of the day. Bombs became a way of life. At first, as soon as the all-clear sounded kids would race to the scene of an explosion to gape with curiosity. Now, just three weeks later, we were thankful that the bombs had fallen on someone else.

Saturday, 7 September 1940, typified this attitude more

than any other day I can remember. My mother had taken me out to buy me a new pair of shoes. While we were in the local market, the sirens sounded. The sky soon filled with smoke as bomb after bomb rained down on the docks less than a mile away. Even as a child, I felt I would be all right. It wasn't me they wanted, it was the docks. The afternoon had begun cloudless and sunny. By five o'clock the sun was blotted out more effectively than by any eclipse and visibility was barely a hundred yards. Great palls of smoke hung ominously trapped between the rows of battle-scarred buildings. Our eyes ran raw. The docks were like a crime-ridden Kasbah. In there, every evil was taking place. But here, just outside, we were safe.

The all-clear sounded around six in the evening. We just had time for a meal before adjourning to the shelter of Aunt Lylie's flat for the night. As the four of us descended our staircase, I began to read a comic that mum had bought me that afternoon.

By now, the evening dusk should have made reading difficult, if not impossible. Yet there I was, a mile from the still-burning docks, easily reading the small print by firelight.

The journey down the street to my aunt's was no more than sixty yards. Even though there was no raid yet in progress, mum insisted that we walked in tight formation. Dad paused momentarily to light a cigarette. 'Oy!' came the cry from Albert Jenkins, the street air-raid warden, 'Put that bloody light out!'

Soon the sirens sounded again. Within minutes the heavy drone of well-laden aircraft could be heard. Explosions punctuated the whole night. This time the docks were by no means exclusive. The bombers were visiting just about everyone. Doors and windows shook and rattled, soot and brick dust cascaded down from the chimney flue and the taste of smoke was everywhere. The incessant assault went on until shortly after daylight, when the all-clear finally sounded.

Everyone was now awake. Indeed, other than the baby, no one had actually slept. Mum had begun to make the tea while dad stretched his legs by walking into my aunt's front room.

'Jack!' he called urgently to my grandfather. 'Come and look at this!' The compulsion in his tone caused everyone to join him. As we looked east through the surprisingly intact window, a whole line of flames formed our riverside horizon.

'Good God,' whispered my mother in hushed tones, 'it looks like the whole world's on fire.'

There was no daylight raid that Sunday. The sheer fury of the onslaught appeared to have exhausted the aggressor as well as the victim. It at least enabled everyone to snatch some sleep before the bombers returned in the evening. Everyone, that is, except the people trapped in the debris, or fighting the fires that still raged all around.

Details of the raids were rarely given on the radio. The announcer would merely say something nondescript such as: 'Enemy planes last night attacked targets in the London area. They were repulsed with heavy losses, and bombs were dropped at random.'

I pointed out to Charlie how lucky we were that we lived in London and not in Random. That unfortunate town seemed to be raided about five times a day. The thing that puzzled me most, however, was just *where* Random was. I assumed that it must be somewhere near London, yet until the start of the blitz I had never heard of it. Charlie, who was quite knowledgeable about these things, said that Random was a town in Essex. Rosie did not think that it could be much of a town, because by now it must have been blown to bits.

We weighed up all of the evidence and mutually decided that perhaps Random was a bigger place than we had given it credit for.

Halfway through October, after Random had suffered another five raids in one day, dad called another family meeting in Aunt Lylie's flat. He asked if anyone now thought we should leave for the country. He said he could sleep at his factory and granddad could still sleep under the table, but everyone else, he thought, should think seriously about leaving London. He pointed out that the raids had been practically continuous now for almost two months. They showed no signs of abating; if anything they were becoming worse. 'To my mind,' he said, 'time is running out for us.'

It seemed like dad had a direct line to Hitler. That night was the worst attack we had yet experienced. In spite of the bombardment, I finally fell asleep, but suddenly I was awoken by the light from the ceiling bulb shining directly into my eyes. 'Come on,' mum was saying, 'move over.' I slowly assembled my wits and was surprised to see, in addition to the room's usual complement, three other familiar-looking people. There, standing just behind mum, was my Uncle George, Aunt Nell and six-year-old cousin, 'Georgie-boy'. Rubbing my eyes, I looked up at the clock. It was five minutes past one! 'Wassamatter?' The six of us already in the bed were, it seemed, to make room for yet one more aunt and cousin. Georgie-boy climbed in the foot of the bed, while Aunt Nell slipped into the top. The bed seemed to bubble with feet.

It transpired that three-quarters of an hour earlier the newcomers had been blasted out of their Kennington flat. They had then walked the two miles, through cascading shrapnel and exploding bombs, to reach us. Slowly the thirteen of us settled down in that kitchen. Someone switched off the light as I turned gingerly away from Aunt Nell's left foot.

At around that moment, on the brewery roof at the end of the street, the local fire-watcher helplessly scanned the sky. Everywhere were exploding shells and bombs. Suddenly he perked up appreciably. It seemed that the guns had achieved at least one success after all! There, caught momentarily in the moonlight, was a parachute. The route it was drifting down should take it squarely on to the roof of Queen's Buildings. If the observer had been in possession of binoculars, he would indeed have seen a parachute. There was, however, no German pilot dangling anxiously on its end, but an eight-feet-long German sea-mine. It was packed with high explosives designed to blast battleships out of the sea. Time had finally run out for Queen's Buildings.

10. Goodbye, Rosie

The explosion* came in two stages. The first woke me instantly, but was all over within a moment. The second seemed to be within my head. I was suddenly aware of an enormous roaring noise, and felt a great pressure inside my skull. Once this effect had worn off – it seemed to take an age but lasted, I suppose, just a few seconds – I began to take stock of the situation. My first reaction was that everyone lying on the floor was dead. In fact, other than some slight lacerations by glass, they were completely unscathed. But there was complete silence in the room. Then I realized that the silence was not confined to the room. Everywhere else was deathly quiet. No doors or windows remained in place in the flat and huge clouds of choking dust had billowed in from outside, but there was not a sound to be heard. Not a cough, not a sigh, not a word, not a moan.

Suddenly noise began to gather momentum as parts of the buildings began to disintegrate. The first of the distant screams then cut through the still night air.

I heard mum's voice call urgently. 'Harry! Stan! Are you all right?'

'Yeh, yeh, ma, fine,' I assured her.

I heard no reply from my brother, although I could feel his legs on mine. The recess in which the bed fitted was too dark to see him.

'Stan!' I called, but there was no answer.

90

I reached out towards his face and discovered a huge chunk of ceiling lying on the pillow. Quickly slipping my hand under the plaster, I was quite surprised to find the space devoid of brother Stanley. I dropped my hand down and felt for his waist. As I ran my fingers quickly up his body, I realized that he had moved in his sleep. His top half was now arched away from me, leaving a space on the pillow between our two heads. It was into this space that the plaster had fallen. He had probably been saved from serious injury by his subconscious aversion to Aunt Nell's feet! I pulled the ceiling plaster to one side and realized that although he was wide awake, he was too terrified to speak.

The room was now coming quickly to life. Dad lifted the heavy balcony door from where it had been blasted against the kitchen table. My grandparents climbed choking out from under it. Urgent voices began to call across the dark room. 'Georgie, are you all right?' 'How's Stella?' 'What's happened? Is everyone okay?' 'I think my hand's cut!' 'Renee, love, where are you!' Suddenly another and more dramatic voice could be heard outside on the staircase. I had heard that bawling voice enough times to recognize it instantly.

'Everyone must leave the building as quickly as possible!' called Albert Jenkins. 'It's beginning to collapse!'

The distant screams grew louder as more and more sections of the tenements fell apart. Each crash of masonry was followed by another great billowing cloud of dust.

'Quick, outside! Don't bother to dress!' ordered dad curtly.

This decree was all very well for the grown-ups, who always slept with their clothes on. But Stan and I and our two girl cousins were all in our nightclothes. I began instinctively to look for my jumper and trousers. The rest of the party assembled themselves with surprising speed and made to join the other tenants who were already filing down the staircase. A serious problem was then discovered. The heavy old door that led on to the staircase had been blown off its hinges. The door frame had also slipped and the door itself was trapped within the twisted frame. The entire weight of the flat above seemed to be bearing down on it. A loud pounding was suddenly heard from outside the door.

'Are you all right in there?' came an unfamiliar voice.

'No, we can't move the door! Can you push against it?' called dad.

'Well, it's a risk, but we'll have to take it!' replied the voice.

This was followed by several loud thuds and suddenly the door burst open. We all looked anxiously up at the ceiling. It creaked but did not move. Standing in the doorway was a giant of a soldier whom none of us had ever seen before.

'Quick, out!' he commanded. 'The buildings are falling apart!' He produced a small pocket torch and shone it rapidly around the room. 'Don't bother to dress, boys,' he said to Stan and me. 'Just get down that staircase as quickly as you can!'

Pyjama-clad, we made to scamper down the old stone steps, but were suddenly restrained by his huge hands.

'You can't walk out with nothing on your feet! There's glass everywhere!'

With that, he picked me up with no effort at all and swung me under his left arm. He repeated the procedure by placing my brother under his right arm. Within a minute, each one of our party had reached the pavement in safety. The soldier handed Stanley over to my mother and placed me down gently on a section of glass-free pavement. I looked up to thank him but he had gone back up the stairs.

It was only then that the sheer desperation of the situation dawned on us. The night was lit by a moon and by searchlights which swept the skies. These lights had locked on to an aeroplane directly overhead. As the guns blasted away, shrapnel fell all over the street like Mrs Williamson's winkleshells.

As the last of the occupants of the block joined us on the pavement, we willingly placed ourselves under the supervision of Albert Jenkins.

'Right, you lot! Make your way around to Charles Dickens School. It's a rest-centre. They'll look after you there. Off you go. I've got work to do here.'

Albert Jenkins undoubtedly revelled in his job as air-raid warden, but it was a job that he was particularly good at. It required a great deal of courage to run up and down a six-storey building in imminent danger of collapse, especially to rescue cantankerous people who had decided not to use the recommended air-raid shelters.

Dad and Uncle George remained behind to help the rescue services and the rest of us moved slowly off in the direction of the school. Our arrival was greeted by a rotund, smiling lady with a huge teapot.

'Have a cup o' tea, loves. Then we'll find you somewhere to sleep.'

Clutching enamelled mugs of scalding tea, we were eventually shown to my very own classroom. Lines of blankets were laid out tidily on the floor.

'Sleep!' echoed Aunt Liz looking wide-eyed all around the room. We were surrounded by glass. There were three huge windows, then a glass partition between us and the next classroom. 'If a bomb goes off here, it'll be like sleeping in a box of razor blades.'

I soon fell asleep. My last waking recollection was of my

mother quietly sobbing into her blanket.

Immediately after a breakfast of watery porridge, Stan and I, together with one or two other night-attired victims, were taken to the clothes table where a great pile of assorted hand-me-downs were waiting for the needy. Eventually, dressed in a pair of tatty corduroy shorts and a baggy jumper, I sat with a pile of children's comics kept in the corner of the classroom and waited for dad and Uncle George to return. As I saw it, my main worry was how to find Rosie and Charlie.

The two men finally returned a little after 9 a.m., having spent the night in a frustrating search for victims. In spite of anxious requests from the women folk, they hardly spoke about their experiences. Not that they needed to, their dirt-covered faces said everything. This questioning of my father made me very agitated. I just knew that I had to return to Queen's Buildings. It was maddening to be so close and yet not know what was going on. Realistically, I also knew that my mother would never permit me to return.

Suddenly I was in with a chance. In an effort to keep the children occupied, one of the voluntary workers had organized a game in the playground.

'Can I go an' play with 'em, ma?' I pleaded.

'You can go into the *playground*, certainly. But you are *not* to go outside! D'you understand that? Not one foot outside!'

'Yes, ma.'

I closed the classroom door behind me and within five minutes had reached Collinson Street. A rope barrier had been placed across the roadway, a short distance from the Buildings, and two stern-faced wardens ensured that nobody passed. They faced a constant barrage of questions from worried enquirers. 'Do you know anything about the people in number twenty-two?' 'Is the lady in twenty-four okay?' 'Where have the survivors been taken?' They answered each question curtly but efficiently.

I stared open-mouthed up at the Buildings. At the brewery end, they were little more than a shell. Floors and ceilings had collapsed, one on the other. The pile of furniture, pets, pianos and people was now two storeys high. Buried somewhere under that cliff-face of masonry was our dog Pie-Shop. The basement shelters, however, should have stood up to the onslaught. That was what they were adapted for. The thick steel and wooden props should have kept the tonnage from falling in on the shelterers below.

Charlie, together with his mother, would have been in the first shelter. Rosie and her family would have been in the second.

I was surprised at the lack of activity around the wreckage. My thoughts seemed to be shared by a tearful, white-faced lady.

'Why is nothing being done? There must still be people trapped in those basement shelters!'

'We can't get at 'em without the whole building collapsing in on us,' explained the warden wearily. 'We're tunnelling through the walls from the basement shelters further down the street. But really it's a total waste of time.'

'What d'you mean, "waste of time"? If there are people in there then they'll still be alive, surely? Those walls are tough and the supports are good. Why is nothing being done?' Her voice rose, emotionally. 'I suppose the wardens have all buggered off somewhere drinking tea or something!'

The warden, whose nerve-ends by now must have been as taut as piano strings, finally broke. 'Nothing is being done because nothing *can* be done! They're all bloody dead! They have drowned! The water main blew instantly and every shelter this end filled with water. They are all sealed in!'

The last vestige of colour drained from the lady's face and she swayed to the ground. As both wardens ran to assist her, I seized the opportunity to duck under the rope. I had covered barely half the distance to the first block when the wardens grabbed me and dragged me back to the barrier – none too kindly, either. I tearfully explained about Rosie and Charlie and they were instantly sympathetic.

'It's no use, son. Everyone who stayed in their flats in these three end-blocks were killed instantly. And those who took shelter in the basements were drowned.'

I sat down on the kerbstone with tears streaming down my face. Poor Charlie, he never did like the water. He would have been so terrified as it climbed up his body. And Rosie – Rosie couldn't possibly be dead. She was life itself! A bouncing, scruffy, dirty-knickered bundle of cheeky fun. Rosie just *had* to be alive. I had never known grief before, I had no idea at all how to combat it.

I wiped my sniffling nose and scuffed my way back to school. I had lost all sense of time and had no idea how long I had been missing. When mum had discovered that I was not in the playground, she had anxiously woken my father. I met him just outside the school gates.

'What's the matter, boy?' he asked softly.

'It's Rosie, dad, Rosie an' Charlie, they're dead!'

'I know, boy, I know. We all know. That's why you weren't allowed to go back to the Buildings.' He put his arm around my baggy jumper.

11. Evacuation

Those days in the rest-centre seemed totally unreal. We all had the feeling that for the victims the war was now over. The blitz no longer seemed anything to do with us. My parents had lost everything they had ever possessed, while I had lost my two best friends and Pie-Shop. That was it, there was nothing more to give. An all-embracing apathy descended upon us. Each night for a week we lay on that school floor surrounded by glass while the bombs rained down. On the whole we slept like logs.

Although we had this feeling of immunity, it was not shared by the staff, who explained that the centre was an emergency service. We had to move on – but where? Aunt Lylie found a space for herself and the baby in a friend's stables which nestled neatly beneath the main railway line near the Elephant and Castle station. My grandparents discovered a damaged but empty flat at the opposite end of Queen's Buildings where, with the help of some plywood and a tarpaulin, some sort of habitation was made. Uncle George and Aunt Nell, together with cousin Georgie-boy, returned to their own locality of Kennington where, they hoped, they would find some sort of shelter. That left six of us – Aunt Liz, her daughter Renee, and the entire Cole family.

'There's now only one thing to do,' said dad firmly to my mother. 'You and the boys will have to go away. I also think that Liz and the baby should go with you.'

This inevitable decision presented no mean problem for my mother. She had been the stumbling block to our evacuation ever since the war had begun. I could see that even now she was seeking some alternative, but there was none.

'Well, perhaps –'

'Perhaps nothing!' snapped dad with unheard-of temper. 'You and the boys are going away to the country and that's the finish of it!' Mum bit her lip but, surprisingly, she neither cried nor argued.

It was shortly after this decision that we received some exciting news. Dad was told that the emergency services had salvaged some of our property from the flat. We all found this quite extraordinary because we thought everything had collapsed into the general wreckage.

'Not so!' said the messenger. 'I don't know what the property is but apparently it is there and it's definitely yours.'

Each of us had a secret wish as to which of our possessions we would most like to be saved. I wanted Pie-Shop or, failing him, my cigarette cards or shrapnel collection. Stan wanted his toy soldiers and his fort. Dad said he would be grateful for just a few pounds, so that he could feel some money in his pocket once more. Mum, predictably and unrealistically, wished for her upright, polished-like-glass, Barnes piano. 'If I got my piano back, perhaps I wouldn't have to go,' she said, hopefully.

We eagerly trooped down to the control centre. There in the back yard was a tiny office. A small, thin, bald man was crouched intently over a huge old ledger. My father explained his business and the man studied a page of the ledger for a minute or so.

'Oh yes, here it is!' He placed his finger on the appropriate entry and moved it across the page. 'You seem to be lucky. There are *two* items for you!'

'Two!' exclaimed dad, now really excited. 'That's marvellous! What are they?'

The man turned slowly on his seat and pointed out of the window with his ancient nibbed pen. 'Well, that's one of them.'

There, propped up against the wall of the outside lavatory and sporting a huge 'Government Property' label, was dad's battered old cycle.

'And here is the other surprise,' announced the man patronizingly.

He handed over to my father a small, badly dented biscuit-tin. Inside was a collection of family photographs that dad had taken with his second-hand box-Brownie.

'Is that it?' demanded mum. 'Nothing else?'

'You've done very well,' reproved the ledger-keeper, leaning back on his chair. 'You have at least received *something* back.'

On Monday of our second week in the centre, dad broke the news that he had fixed himself up with a bunk bed at his factory; the rest of us were to leave the following day. At that stage he did not know where we were going. All he had been told was that it was somewhere in the country, a great distance from London. We were to assemble at Liverpool Street station the very next morning.

Liverpool Street was one of London's grimiest stations. Soot festooned the walls and the smell of smoke and railway engines pervaded every corner. Like all wartime railway stations, it had an aura all of its own. It was a place of transition where people paused just before their whole lives were changed. Sometimes for the better, sometimes for the worse. Even as a child I felt this change of direction. I just knew that life would never be quite the same again.

I felt alone and totally bewildered.

We gathered on a platform with families from all over London. Each of us had been provided with a packed lunch, but still had no idea where we were bound, or how long we were to be on the train. When finally our train steamed in, we joined in the undignified scramble for seats. There were a few yells and a distant whistle. Then, with a rapid tattoo of muffled power, the first creak was heard as the train eased forward. We waved frantically to my father from the window. Then, with increasing momentum, we rounded the first bend out of Liverpool Street station. Bomb-damaged roofs began to slip past our vision, their broken slates shining in the steadily falling rain. Soon the word was whispered from carriage to carriage: 'We're going to Norfolk – but don't tell anyone – it's a secret destination!' Just why it was supposed to be such a secret, nobody asked. And there was one other thing that bothered us – where the bloody hell *was* Norfolk?

The hundred-mile journey from Liverpool Street to King's Lynn took precisely nine hours. I could have cycled it faster. Delay followed delay. Whenever the train stopped – and it did so dozens of times – so the rumours escalated. I finally had the impression that the whole of the Nazi war-machine had been geared for no other reason than to prevent me leaving London.

The reception committee at King's Lynn was just as tired and irritable as we were. They too had been waiting half the day for that faltering train to arrive. They herded us quickly into a fleet of Eastern County buses and we were soon transported to the village school at Wootton, some three miles away. There we were split into groups of varying sizes and about twenty of us were allocated to the village of Gayton some six miles distant.

Within minutes of arriving at Gayton village school the

100

most degrading moment of our lives took place. We were asked to stand up in a line. Wearily climbing to our feet, we all obliged. Then several people who had been sitting around in the rear classroom came forward and began to stare at us. One by one, they approached a tweed-suited lady who sat at a desk with a register in front of her, pointed at one of the families in the line and whispered in the lady's ear. Each time, she nodded and asked the name of the family that had been pointed at.

'Brown.'

'Very well then, Mrs Brown, you have been billeted with Mrs Dawson here. If you would be so kind as to take hold of your children, Mrs Dawson will take you to her home.'

We had been put on display and offered for selection!

In twos and threes, our line gradually dissolved, Aunt Liz and Renee being among the first to be claimed. As each prospective host stared up and down the line and then made their choice, so our sense of rejection became more acute. Finally just three evacuees remained: mum, Stan and me. We looked anxiously at the last of the choosers: an elderly silver-haired lady, with just a remote air of elegance about her. At first glance she appeared strict, yet this impression was not borne out by the kindly twinkling eyes.

'No, I'm very sorry,' said the old lady to my mother, 'but we only have room for a mother and a baby. We did make this clear right from the beginning.' She turned her head in a reproachful glance towards the tweed-suited supervisor.

'Oh please!' begged mum. 'Please take us in. I assure you we'll be no trouble.'

'I would willingly do so, my dear, but I only have one spare bed and it is not very big. I cannot see how you would manage.'

'Please!' repeated mum, now very close to tears. 'Please just give us a chance.'

The old lady looked at my mother sympathetically for a few seconds and instinctively reached down and placed her left hand on my brother's head, ruffling his hair. 'Well, if you wouldn't mind all sharing the same bed, you are more than welcome,' she relented.

'Thank you, Mrs Robinson,' said the tweed-suited lady. 'That concludes the billeting for today. It's all worked out rather well, really.'

Mrs Robinson took hold of my brother's hand and led us out of the school and back to her home. By that act she started a relationship that survived for over forty years.

12. Norfolk family Robinson

Mrs 'Granny' Robinson lived with her son Baden and her daughter Polly in a quiet semi-detached house in the middle of Gayton village. The old lady had been the mother of a large farming family, but widowhood and the marriage of most of her children meant she now lived quietly in retirement. Polly was a small, quick individual, full of nervous energy. Baden, on the other hand, was a powerful, slow-moving man, with arms like tree trunks. Just how these quite different people, all comfortably set in their ways, opened their hearts to three total strangers amazes me still.

Next morning, the crowing of Baden's cockerels awakened me from several layers of sleep. It took a little time to assemble my thoughts. The sun had driven away the rain of yesterday and was streaming into the bright, compact room. I eased myself out of bed and tip-toed to the small window. A long garden, still full of autumn vegetables, sloped away from the house. A fenced chicken-run bisected it halfway along its length. It was not yet seven o'clock but already Polly was feeding the chickens and Baden was inspecting his winter cabbage. A neighbour, similarly engaged with her poultry, called cheerfully over to Polly. Beyond the garden and away from the village, a flock of gulls followed a ploughing tractor. The terrain then sloped gently up to a clump of fir trees, perched on a low hill some three miles away. My first impression was one of peace and quiet but muted noises began to reach my ears. Chickens, tractors, gulls, soft Norfolk voices and the sound that I was to associate forever with East Anglia – the kraar-kraaring of carrion-crows.

By 8.30 a.m. we had breakfasted and washed and mum was planning our first day. It was decided – not by me – that I must begin school as soon as possible.

'He's got so much to catch up on,' said mum worriedly to Polly.

Gayton school was a grey, stone and brick, one-storey building with two classrooms. Together with a dozen or so other evacuees, we were enrolled that morning and began school immediately. Stan went into Miss Dobson's infant class, while I went into the top class under the watchful eye of teacher and headmaster, one William Jenner.

William Jenner, or 'Old Buff' as he was always called, except to his face, was an astonishing man, first because he had managed to obtain the post of teacher in the first place, and second because he had actually remained in office for almost fifteen years during which time no child from the school had ever passed a scholarship to any form of higher education. He was a huge man with a huge stomach. He had been a regular soldier in the Royal East Kent Regiment (nicknamed 'The Buffs') and had seen service in the Boer war, the 1914–18 war and had also been on the small, unsuccessful expeditionary force to Northern Russia in 1919.

Under Old Buff's direction, pupils spent many school hours working in the large school garden, for the headmaster also owned a greengrocer's shop in King's Lynn! In the three years that I remained in his class, he never once taught a scholastic lesson. There was, however, one subject that he would discuss incessantly during school hours: battle campaigns. He was obsessed by them. Maps of every theatre of war adorned all four classroom walls. Each morning for two hours he would lead the children of Gayton Church School through the intricate long-term strategy of the Allied Chiefs of Staff. At the age of ten I could draw every mile of North African coastline. I not only knew small towns and villages but base-dumps and minefields. After the German attack on Russia, I was more familiar with the Pripet marshes than ever I was with the Lake District. In that damp school classroom, we fought guerrilla-warfare and tank battles. We negotiated minefields and convoy strikes. We foiled Hitler, Mussolini and, a year later, Tojo.

The days in the classroom fell roughly into three sections. The first hour was taken up with reading a Church Catechism, a small booklet mainly provided for study by those intending to become confirmed within the church. We were never actually taught anything from this book, we simply had to read it each day for an hour. The remaining two hours of the morning would be taken up with our military studies. In the afternoon, weather permitting, we would work in the garden. During the bad weather we would remain in class and read to ourselves. This afternoon reading and the morning catechism were carried out in absolute silence.

Jenner would sit at his desk and study his *Daily Mail*, occasionally raising an eye to a distant corner of the room. If anything untoward caught his eye, either real or imaginary, he would utter the fated words, 'C'mon here!' No name would ever accompany this command and the two words were as irrevocable as any verdict by the Inquisition. Two chairs would be heard sliding back. The first was that of the unfortunate miscreant and the second would be the headmaster's. Having carefully folded his *Daily Mail*, he would then slowly walk the three paces to the old brown store-cupboard. From the top shelf he would remove the heavy cane that had stood him in such good stead for all of his years at the school. The rest of the class would then happily raise their eyes from their books in order to enjoy the pain and discomfort of a much-loved friend.

He 'paid no special attention to evacuees except if a visitor came to the school. Then he would display us like pet serfs. 'Stand up all evacuees,' he would boom. 'And *stand still*!' We would remain motionless while the visitors looked us up and down with genuine curiosity. I think I always expected them to examine our teeth and make a bid for us. On the command, 'Evacuees, sit down,' we would return to the anonymity of our desks.

We had been at Gayton for barely three months when my mother decided that air-raids or no air-raids, her place was in London with my father. Both mum and dad came to see us every couple of months or so, but to my brother and me these visits slowly came to mean less and less. Stan had really taken to Baden by now and followed him about everywhere. Granny and Polly between them were perfect surrogate mothers, providing for his every need.

I was at a more difficult age to adjust. I could not accept our hosts, marvellous though they were, as parents; on the other hand, my real parents were now distant figures whose occasional weekend visits always seemed to prevent me from doing far more interesting things with my new friends in the village. This situation caused a great slackening in my emotional ties with my parents.

Although my mother had returned to London, Aunt Liz and Cousin Renee were still quite happily billeted in the village, and my aunt soon announced her intention of marrying a local farmworker. Barry, her intended, was one of a large family from the other end of the village. He was an amiable man with a ready smile, a grip of iron, and a Norfolk accent one could cut with a knife.

This new family relationship had one great bonus for me: one of Barry's brothers assembled bicycles from spares as a paying hobby, and through him I finally managed to secure my very own bike. This at last put me on an equal footing with my schoolmates and, indeed, virtually the whole population of Norfolk – everyone in those days cycled. I do not think anything has ever given me greater pleasure than that bike. I was hardly ever off it. I cycled everywhere. When on her marriage my aunt moved to a tied cottage near the royal estate of Sandringham, I frequently rode over on a Sunday. Regretfully, this was not due to any great family loyalty but mainly because of the fish-stocked stream that ran through the approaches to her house.

On each of my cycling excursions, I ventured further and further afield. The peacetime resort of Hunstanton, some twenty miles away, was a particular draw, not because it was such a wonderful place, but because it was out-of-bounds to all visitors. That made it a must. However, the most important attractions of all were the air-bases. During the war, the flat Norfolk countryside had practically become one vast airfield. Crashes often happened in these crowded skies, usually caused by brand new darting fighters colliding with each other in mid-air. Once, while on the way to my aunt's, I was showered by pieces of tail-plane that fell through some low rolling clouds. A distant explosion a few minutes later told its own story.

Now at last I was beginning to feel like a lad of the village. Being accepted had not proved easy, but it helped that I was keen on games: I was eager to play either cricket or football for just as long as anyone wished to kick or throw me a ball, and this soon made me one of a group.

There was, however, one solitary six-second achievement that evaded me for months. I knew that once I could accomplish this test I would be established for the duration of the war among the boys of the school. On a small hill just to the north of the village was a disused lime-kiln. The large, horseshoe-shaped excavations had bitten deep into the side of the hill. A high hedge surrounded the kiln, and within that confine the tall grasses and bushes grew unchecked. A small army could have hidden there. It was, of course, a superb place to play. Poised on the edge of the white-faced cliff was a short but sturdy elder tree. Its tangled roots filtered through the top few feet of cliff face and its small branches overhung the sheer drop to the diggings far below. Hanging from the thickest of these branches, some five feet out from the cliff face, was a heavy old iron chain. This chain had doubtless served some function long ago but it now hung forlorn and still, too heavy to stir itself even in the strongest of breezes.

This final sporting test required a boy to spring along the path that led to the elder tree – itself a precarious task, with numerous roots waiting to snare the unwary – and jump off the cliff, five feet out into space, and seize the chain. For this accomplishment to be satisfactorily performed, he would need to have a firm grip, a head for heights and, above all, a sense of direction! Once the jumper had gripped the chain, the test was virtually over. All he then had to do was slide to the bottom – and finish!

I must have raced at that tree scores of times. Sometimes I fell over the roots, sometimes I didn't. Yet always there was a different reason for not attempting the jump. 'The sun was in my eyes,' was a favourite one. A strange phenomenon this, since the jump faced north-east. 'My boot is falling off.' (I wore wellington boots with two pairs of socks; even in ideal conditions they took five minutes to remove.) Or I would point out to any doubting spectators that I was jumping with a great disability: my old war-wound, sustained while pulling an orphaned baby from a burning blitzed building, was giving me gyp.

Finally, one wonderful Saturday morning, I did it. I have no idea just how I did it, I just ran up, jumped, then it was all over. It must have been a little like suicide.

The jump from the cliff and the possession of my bicycle were the real turning points of my whole evacuation. I had no need to return to London now, I was finally accepted here.

13. Brenda and two rats

Although the financial needs of a young evacuee boy in a sweetless, toyless, wartime countryside were minimal, the occasional shilling was gratefully received. So when one playtime at school it was suggested that I join a few other boys that evening in approaching a local farmer for a harvest job, I was keen.

There were very few small farms in the Gayton area, most of the acreage being divided between just two big landowners: Easter's to the south of the village and Hotson's to the north. Easter's was the most sought after, because the rate of pay for boys was infinitely superior to that of his rival. Needless to say, by the time that I applied Easter's had their full quota of staff, so I offered my services to Alf Dunwood, the foreman at Hotson's.

'So you want a 'arvest job, do you, boy?' he asked, looking me intently up and down. 'Oi didn't think you Londoners knew very much aboot 'arvestin'. Still, if you're prepared to work, Oi'll give yer a job. Start Monday week, a' seven in the mornin'. An' you'd better fetch plenty of food 'cause you won't be finishin' until nigh on nine o'clock a' night. Roight, off you go an' don't y'be late, understand?'

Monday week dawned bright and sunny and Polly woke me at six o'clock with tea and porridge. As I left the house at a quarter to seven, she gave me an enormous packet of sandwiches and a bottle of sugarless, milkless tea. 'It may take you a while to get used to it,' she said, 'but once you do, you will find it very refreshing.' She was right on both counts. It took me two weeks before I could drink the stuff, but once I did, it was excellent.

All of the boys were met by Alf Dunwood who gave us a quick briefing. 'Git the hosses out of the stable an' saddle 'em. Then we'll put 'em in the carts. Oi'll show you the once, but after that, you'll be doin' it on your own, understand?'

I was eleven years of age when I first attempted to slip a collar over a reluctant farm horse, I was fully aware by then of all the the swear words in common usage, but I had no idea how easy it was to string them all together. That was until I balanced that damned collar. On my very first morning in the stables I came blasphemously of age. With just more than a little collective help, the huge shires were eventually saddled, harnessed and secured between the sloping shafts of the two-wheeled carts. Then the eight carts, each with a complement of two men and a boy, who was balanced precariously on the horse, left the farmyard in a slow-moving convoy.

The task of most boys at harvest time was purely to sit on the back of the horse, yelling at the top of his voice. The carts would be driven around the fields collecting up the sheaves of corn that had been stacked in heaps. One man would walk alongside the cart, tossing sheaves on to it with a pitchfork while the other stood inside the cart loading the sheaves. The skill was to carry as many sheaves as possible without the load falling off the cart. All of the loading skill in the world, however, would count for nothing unless the boy riding the horse avoided every hole, rut and ridge in the fields. Because of the size of these loads, loader and boy were frequently out of sight of one another. The boy would therefore be required to give ample warning of any deviation, by yelling out, 'Hol-gee' (a contraction of 'Hold-tight'). All and sundry referred to us as the 'Hol-gee boys'.

Once the load had reached a maximum safe height, another hol-gee boy would arrive with an empty cart. The lads would then swop and the fully laden cart would be driven away to the distant cornstack. The two-and-a-half-man team would then repeat the whole operation.

At nine o'clock that evening, I cycled home weary and hungry but also very happy. I had really enjoyed my first day at work.

Each day thereafter was very much the same, except during the wet weather when we would all go 'hedging and ditching'. Occasionally a horse would lose a shoe which meant a trip to the blacksmith's. For me, this was the highlight of the entire harvest period. The smells and sounds of the blacksmith's shop were an absolute delight. The roaring bellows, the clanging anvil and the hissing hot irons amalgamated into a rich cacophony of sounds. Dan Rogers the blacksmith was a cheery old soul who constantly sang his own variations of old country songs. Many of his lyrics were questionable in the extreme. He managed to incorporate the two lines:

> As she lay in sweet repose
> the vicar's hand slipped up her clothes

into the verse of any traditional song from 'The Lincolnshire Poacher' to 'Londonderry Air'.

Changing my employer, I spent the next two harvests working happily at Easter's, but in addition to this, I could regularly sound out the foreman for any extra seasonal work that might be on offer. This work ranged from mangling turnips and swedes for cattle food, to 'beating'

112

for the pheasant shoots.

Swede-mangling turned out to be a definite step on my ladder of life's experience. This particular task had to be performed for a couple of hours each evening after school, for about four weeks, and I shared the work with big Brenda, the farm's own Land Army girl. The Women's Land Army of around 80,000 volunteers had been mobilized at the outbreak of war. They could be directed to work anywhere in the country and wore an easily recognizable uniform of brown corduroy breeches and a dark green jumper. Just as soon as the war began, Brenda had thrown up her employment as a secretary in London and had taken instantly to farm life.

The usual routine was for each of us to work on the mangle for around fifteen minutes in turn. At first I took a couple of comics to read during my rest period, but after a while I lost interest in the adventures of Pansy Potter and the life of Keyhole Kate and became fascinated by Brenda instead. Brenda was extremely popular with the farm hands, both for her personality and for her rather obvious physical characteristics. However, she was basically a shy girl and rather suspicious of their intentions – probably with very good reasons.

During the hours that we spent together in that shed, she confided in me all her hopes and fears. It was painfully clear to me that she saw no potential threat from a comic-reading, thirteen-year-old boy. Now I may have posed no threat for Brenda, but she certainly posed one, or more accurately two, for me. It was the mangle that did it. To pull that mangle up to the top of its circuit required the deepest of breaths and a very open chest. It was at this stage in Brenda's stint that I always stopped looking at my comic. I was paid fifteen shillings per week for the five evenings of work, yet in truth I would have done it for nothing.

When some months later, we again worked together, the occasion turned out to be both memorable and unbearable.

The threshing machine was making its annual round of West Norfolk and had arrived at the village farms. Threshing was the one farm task that I really disliked. No matter how we buttoned or tied our clothing, particles of dust, soot and corn-chaff would still enter. Eyes, ears and nostrils would be found out within minutes and one would rub, scratch and sneeze for the rest of the day. The only part of it that I remotely enjoyed was when the last few sheaves were lifted from the base of the stack. Apart from signalling the end of the work, it was then time for the rats to run. Before work on the stack had begun, a fine-mesh wire would have been staked some two feet high all around it. As the men started to remove the top layers of sheaves, so the vermin sought refuge lower and lower down the stack. As soon as those last few sheaves were lifted, so they would run for new cover. Usually the gamekeeper would be in attendance with a pair of his best ratting terriers. The subsequent slaughter would therefore be horrendous. With the cheers of the man exciting the dogs to even greater carnage, the dying rats would emit the most penetrating of squeals as they hurled themselves against the unyielding fence.

Once in a while, the gamekeeper would be unpardonably absent from this slaughter. Then it would be a time for thick sticks and heavy boots, as everyone was expected to leap the fence and join in the fray. One golden rule for every man in this situation was never to leave his trouser bottoms flapping. A sanctuary-seeking rat up his corduroyed legs could well put a fellow on tip-toe for the rest of his life. As many as two hundred vermin might be slaughtered at the completion of a cornstack threshing. Young boys would then wander around the battlefield, eagerly turning over corpses in a search for the largest. This king-rat would be proudly displayed for a day or so, like some prize salmon. The rest would be burnt or buried.

My working reunion with Brenda took place on one of these threshing days. Brenda and I reluctantly shared the dirtiest job of the whole threshing operation: keeping the waste chutes cleared. When at last the corn stack had been threshed and all the rats destroyed, we tried to forget our discomfort by joining the rest of the hands for our lunch break. One or two of the younger men, having finally satisfied their appetite for food, began to tell coarse jokes – none of which I fully understood – in voices deliberately loud enough for Brenda to hear. My ignorance of their humour did not of course prevent me from joining in the gales of masculine laughter that followed each punchline. Finally the most daring of them, a tough-looking curly-haired lad, broke into an old farm ditty whose blatant double-meaning was obvious even to me:

> Come into the barn where we cannot be seen
> an' I'll show you the works o' my threshin'
> machine . . .

As the young men well knew, Brenda could only be teased so far before she would finally erupt.

'Why you dirty little sod,' she glowered. 'I wouldn't go into a barn with you even when you are grown up into a man!'

The rest of the hands cheered this snub greatly. The young man, realizing that the girl would almost certainly come off best in any verbal exchange, then turned physical. Climbing to his feet, he picked up the still warm king-rat by its great tail and advanced on the sitting Brenda.

'Come on, then, gal, how'd you like to 'ave this 'ere

little fella down your neck?'

I do not think that anyone present really thought that he would carry out his threat. In fact I doubt if he even intended to. He probably thought that Brenda would run away screaming. Brenda, however, was not a fleeing screamer. She was a stand-and-fighter.

'You wouldn't dare!' she hissed, which, in the circumstances, was just about the worst possible thing to have uttered.

The youth faltered for a moment, just a pace in front of her. He was desperately seeking a way out. Without an audience, there would have been no problem. But at least a dozen people were present, all wondering how he could best get off the hook that he so clumsily had made for himself. For a moment, it looked like some pagan ritual. The young man stood feet astride, staring at the girl, the rat ominously swinging backward and forward. The girl, on the other hand, sat defiantly looking up at him, her head roughly level with his groin. I was too frightened to say a word but I willed her desperately to climb to her feet. If she would just stand on her feet she was in with a chance. Appeasement, however, was not a word in Brenda's vocabulary. She turned her head deliberately towards me and pointed at the dead vermin still swinging in the young man's hand.

'Look at that one, Harry, that's the more intelligent of the two rats.'

The youth finally had nowhere to hide and he knew it. He was on to her in a flash. He dropped the rat alongside her, then with his right hand pulled her head forward into his groin. With his left hand he seized the back of her jumper and gaped it open at the neck. Locking her head firmly between his corduroy thighs, he again picked up the dead rat, this time with his now freed right hand. The creature was so big that it took three great heavy thrusts to ram its furry, blood-soaked body down the back of the girl's green jumper. Even then, some ten inches of greasy black tail protruded.

In spite of the prolonged build-up to the situation, Brenda had been slow to realize just how badly out of hand it was. But the feel of greasy fur on her flesh galvanized her into action. Suddenly she pummelled with her fists and bit deeply into the crotch of the youth's trousers. He leapt back screaming.

Ted Darling, the farm charge-hand, at long last decided to enter the proceedings: 'Come on, the pair o' you. It's all gettin' rather silly. I think you'd better stop before someone gets hurt, don't you?'

Although I thought the young man had now come off very much the worse, my allegiance was still with Brenda. I grabbed the tail of the rat and endeavoured to pull it out from the jumper. The claws, however, must have been catching on the woollen fibres. Sensing my difficulty, Brenda swiftly crossed her arms and both lifted and shook the sides of her jumper. The creature swung momentarily on a couple of threads, before plunging head first to the damp soil. It lay for a moment in an absurd upside-down pose before slowly rolling over to the more dignified 'dead' position. Just before her jumper fell back to her waist, I had caught a split second's glimpse of her bare back.

'Brenda! You're bleedin'!' I blurted out.

'Am I? Quickly, come with me!' she commanded.

Pulling me by the hand, she sprinted towards the open field-gate. We dashed across the Norwich Road and sidled our way through the thick hedge opposite. Beyond this hedge lay a copse where hazel-nuts grew in an autumn abundance. In the middle of the copse was a small reed-covered water-pit. A flurry of moorhens plopped quickly into the water. Once we were well into the wood, she turned her back and bent forward again, raising her jumper.

'Touch each of the places where I'm bleeding,' she ordered from over her shoulder.

I placed my filthy hands in the thickly smeared blood and gingerly moved my fingers exploratively over her smooth back.

'You ain't bleedin' from anywhere, Bren. It must 'ave been the rat's blood!'

'Are you sure? Check again.'

'Yeh, Bren, I'm positive. There's nothin' on your back at all, 'cept you.'

She looked thoughtful for a moment. Then, having planned out her movements, she quickly listed them.

'Listen, Harry. You keep a good lookout for any peepers who might creep through the woods. I'm going to clean up. What with that stinking rat and the threshing machine, I feel absolutely rotten.'

Then, without any attempt at additional cover, she began to peel off her clothes. Her sudden movement made me burn with embarrassment. I hastily turned away to face the edge of the wood in a futile search for peepers. The way I felt, the only peeper that Brenda was in any danger from was already there in the wood with her! Even though my head had now turned dutifully away, my eyes were revolving frantically. My brain appeared to be sending out two contrasting messages. The first, to my head, said that it must not look. The second, to my eyes, demanded that I did. However, my head was now directed towards the road and would not budge. Even my ears seemed out of control. After a minute or so, they picked up the soft alluring sound of gently splashing water. The excitement was further reinforced by the soft female gasp as the same chill water touched bare warm flesh. Just as the whole situation was becoming far too intoxicating for any susceptible thirteen-year-old to cope with, the bubble burst. An exclamation from the fair Brenda shattered my romantic illusions to fragments.

'Sod this water! It's full of cow-shit!'

This oath broke the spell for me. I turned quite casually to face her. She was already smoothing down both her jumper and her hair.

'Come on, Harry, let's go and see what sort of damage I inflicted on that sod's manhood.'

14. Back home

Some days later we were halfway through breakfast when I realized that neither Granny Robinson nor Polly was speaking. They both sat and watched us tearfully, as my brother and I tucked into our porridge.

'What's the matter, Polly? Is something wrong?' I asked.

She slid a crumpled brown envelope across the table towards me.

'There's a letter from your mother.' She paused and bit her lip and looked protectively towards my brother. 'She wants you both home.'

'Home! When? Where?'

'She wants you both back in London – and she's coming for you tomorrow!'

I found the idea of moving back to London difficult to take in. Certainly I had wondered from time to time what life would be like in that ravaged city, but Gayton was now my home. Where would 'home' be in London? Queen's Buildings, or certainly our part of them, had been long destroyed. Where would we live? Mum had mentioned in her letters that they now had a flat somewhere in Southwark, but I had never really taken much interest. For the first time since I had set foot in the village – almost three years to the day – I felt really unhappy.

'I'm goin' down to the school at playtime, Polly. I want to tell all the kids that I'm leavin'.'

It was beginning to rain as I entered the school

playground but everyone seemed to be playing busily. I announced my impending departure in as casual a voice as I could manage. I think I expected everyone to be absolutely devastated at the news. In reality no one took a blind bit of notice. 'Okay, see yer soon,' was about as close as I got to an impassioned plea to stay. When at last the interval whistle caused the children to file chatteringly back into school, I experienced a gut-thumping feeling of loss. I walked head-down out of the playground and, to my astonishment, tears streamed down my face. Because there was no possibility of taking my cycle back to London – but primarily because I was still crying – I decided to go for one last ride around the surrounding villages. Somehow the steady rain did not seem to matter. As Baden would have said: 'A drop o' rain ain't goin' to hurt you, boy, you ain't goin' to shrink!'

On balance, and despite the sadness at leaving, I think I felt that London was after all where I belonged. During the next twenty-four hours my mother questioned me repeatedly and I always opted to return – but it was close.

The next day we made a painful farewell to the wonderful Robinsons and caught the noon bus to King's Lynn. It was long after ten o'clock before we had creaked into King's Cross, and we had to rush to catch the last underground train home. With my brother wandering dozily behind us, we struggled down the gloomy staircase to the underground platform far below. Everywhere were sleeping bodies. Our rattling train called at six stations, each packed with hundreds of people all living on the platform within the confines of white painted lines which allowed just the minimum of space for passengers to come and go. Many shelterers were reading or playing cards; others were holding discussions or singing; some just slept. At each station, as our train door slid open, a cocktail of body odour and strong carbolic wafted aggressively into our compartment.

It was obvious to me that most of the passengers on the train despised the shelterers. I later realized that a 'deep shelter' mentality had taken root among some Londoners. Each morning when they woke, their prime aim was to ensure their return that evening into the safe bowels of the city's underground system. So obsessive did many of them become that some families allocated one of their number to remain in a queue all day in order to obtain a place for the evening. These people became mole-like, almost afraid of the daylight itself.

It was three years since I had last seen the metropolis, yet even in the pitch dark of the black-out I could sense the change. When I had left London in 1940, the war had been an adventure. Now, in 1943, it was a way of life.

Our new home was at Aylesford House, five minutes from the Borough underground station and just a few yards from where I had seen the violent Mosley march some six years earlier. We occupied a flat on the top floor of a four-storey block that had been completed at the outbreak of war. Already great cracks scarred the walls as a result of nearby bomb blasts. Yet, all in all, Aylesford House had survived rather well. In comparison to Queen's Buildings the new flat was palatial. It consisted of three rooms and a kitchen, plus a bathroom and an *indoor* toilet!

As we wearily climbed the sixty-four stairs to our flat, we were met by my father scampering down them. He was a sensitive man who, like many from his background, found emotions confusing. He would deliberately hide them behind a soft, agreeable humour. A wartime reunion with his two sons after an intermittent separation of three years simply threw him into bewilderment. He would have been longing for the next day when the trauma of our reunion would be over. Then he could be his real self and act as if we had never been away.

My father had been called up for military service but having reported to his unit he was immediately sent back to his factory which made and mended flying suits. He was a skilled furrier, and repairing the bullet holes in some dead gunner's jacket was considered essential to the morale of the next young flyer it was to adorn. I knew that even though he was nearing forty, he felt quite guilty about the deferment of his military service. In an effort to placate his conscience, he joined the Home Guard, spending two or three full nights a week manning an anti-aircraft rocket gun in the local park.

It was German policy at the time to stage 'nuisance raids', in which a solitary plane would approach the capital causing the sirens to sound and the guns to open fire. Six million people living in and around the city would then rouse from their slumbers, leave their beds and feel their way into dark, damp shelters. Within minutes the raider would have turned tail and fled back across the Channel, having successfully ruined yet another night's sleep for the capital's workforce. Sometimes this practice was repeated twice or even three times a night.

One of these raids took place on our very first night back in London. Barely twenty minutes after we had fallen into the shelter, the slow early whine of the 'all-clear' began. People gathered up their belongings and filed chattering out into the still dark night. A collection of goodnights were called and most made their way back to a hopefully still-warm bed.

'Right, get some sleep, you two,' ordered mum. 'You're both going back to school tomorrow.'

I was taken aback at this. Somehow it had never

occurred to me that we would ever return to school again. I lay awake until dawn when I heard my father's key slide into the front door lock. It seemed quite strange to see him in uniform. There was barely time to swop stories of our first raid before he was off again, this time to the factory. Not only did my father work there, but also my mother, three aunts, two uncles and a cousin. Because the family seemed so well represented, I tentatively offered my services in lieu of school. Mum was having none of it, however. 'You've run wild once during this bloody war and it's not happening again. You are well due some schooling m'lad.' She glanced up at the clock. 'In two hours' time to be precise.'

I sighed. Still, there were only nine months to go then I could leave forever. I was not sure which I was looking forward to most, the end of the war or the end of my schooling. They had both been a disaster.

My teacher at Snowfields London County Council Elementary School was Mr Lynn ('Old Lynnie'), who taught us every subject except singing. With the exception of Miss Jones at Charles Dickens, no other teacher made such an impression on me as did Mr Lynn. For the first time in my life I understood the meaning of the description 'gentleman'. In local parlance, Old Lynnie was a real toff.

A survivor of the 1916 battle of the Somme, Mr Lynn encapsulated for me everything that I realized I admired. He was a smartly dressed, silver-haired man, square of build and a little above average height. He spoke with the gentlest of rural accents and was tolerant to an extreme. No matter what the argument he would always see, and urge others to see, the opposing point of view. In addition to this, his ruddy face was rarely without a wide smile. I was led to understand that there were schools where they had a different teacher for every subject. Well, we didn't need one. We had Mr Lynn, and Mr Lynn simply knew everything.

It was during my last term at school that yet another exodus from London began. Within two weeks of the Allied landing in Normandy, which we hoped would bring the war to its final stage, an awful new Nazi weapon made its debut: flying bombs, specially designed to crash in the centre of our city. After a brief family meeting, brother Stan was returned swiftly to Norfolk. I was determined to stay in London this time, primarily because I was due to leave school once and for all within a few weeks. Mister Lynn, sad to say, had arrived just too late in my life.

At their peak, dozens of these flying bombs, or 'doodle-bugs', roared in every day. They were sinister little things to look at as they droned, then spluttered, their way across the capital. As long as they droned they were usually safe. It was when they spluttered or, even more dangerously, cut out altogether that they were lethal. In that event, you had to get down, down just as low as you could go. If you were caught in the open street, then the gutter was the only place to be. You buried yourself there, with your face pushed into the crevice of the kerbstone and the road. Then you prayed. When the explosion finally ripped through an adjacent area, you would realize thankfully that it was some other bugger who had reluctantly copped it. You would give a quick sigh of relief, do your best to help, and then go about your normal business as if nothing had happened.

In spite of these new regular flying bomb attacks, most people adjusted their lives astonishingly well. On the other hand, I found it particularly difficult to keep up the momentum of my schooling during its last few weeks. I carried out the usual pretences, but reality was very close.

What was I going to do when I left school, for example?

Then, during Monday playbreak of my last week at school, Mr Lynn kept me back in class and asked what job I had planned to take up. On discovering my dilemma, he studied me thoughtfully for a minute or so. Then quite casually he murmured, 'Tell me, how do you think you would feel about working with Miss Brock's sister?'

Miss Brock was one of my favourite teachers, so the idea instantly appealed to me. 'Her sister! You bet, sir! I think that would be really smashin'.'

'Hang on a minute, boy, it may not be all that "smashin'"'. You have no idea what sort of job it is yet. She wants someone to work in an office with her.'

My spirits fell just a little at this. Office work had never entered my list of possibilities. But I raced home that evening and breathlessly broke the news to my parents. 'It's one of the teachers from school, mum. She's specially asked for me and she wants to know if dad could call in at the office for a chat.'

Mum was impressed. Two days later, when dad arrived at the office and clapped eyes on Miss Brock's sister, *he* was impressed.

'Well, the job has tremendous prospects,' she told him. 'Of course, being a shipping firm it's a bit quiet at the moment, but once this war is over then your son will be all over Europe.'

Dad was really taken by this. The only member of our family who had ever travelled in his civilian job was Uncle Tim – and he was a coalman. 'All over Europe, eh?' echoed my father. 'Yes, I like the sound of that.'

I had just a few days to prepare for work and, according to my parents, required two essential items before I could start. First, I needed a suit. 'When you work in an office,' pointed out dad, 'you must always be presentable. After all, you'll probably be working with the guv'nor!' Dad was always in total awe of office staff and 'guv'nors' in particular. 'No one from our family has ever worked in an office before,' beamed mum proudly. The second required item was a second-hand cycle. 'You must always be on time for work,' lectured dad. To be late for work was the greatest crime in my father's calendar. He had never been late in his entire working life. My brother and I were to be tragic disappointments to him.

15. Charterhouse

The cinema had become a tremendous draw for me. Even at the height of the flying bomb campaign, there were five cinemas within a ten minutes' walk of our flat. All had special Sunday showings and at least two of them changed their programme three times a week. This meant that it was possible to see no fewer than twelve film programmes within the space of seven days! Time and finances allowing.

Since I was still a child, there were certain films that I could see only if accompanied by an adult. My parents were not great cinema lovers, so the only way round this problem was to stand outside the picture house and ask to be taken in by the first amenable adult. Of course the staff all knew of this practice – they could hardly have failed to notice a whole queue of youngsters loitering at their doors – but they accepted it. After all, the law made no stipulation about parents, just 'adults'.

Even the youngest of us was aware of one danger, however. Occasionally the film would be interrupted by a sudden commotion and a soprano-voiced boy yelling, 'Oy! You dirty old sod!' The more experienced of us would avoid this problem by separating from our escort just as soon as we were inside the auditorium. I carried out this drill religiously with men but it simply never dawned on me to be on guard against women. That was until I saw *Madonna of the Seven Moons*. Then the plump matronly type who had pleasantly escorted me in and fed me two cough sweets turned out to be no Madonna. She had two buttons off my flies before the credits had finished rolling!

Soon, though, I realized that I no longer needed the company of an adult: I had discovered an infallible passport. On my fourteenth birthday I had inherited an old overcoat from my Uncle Sid, who had died some years before. This garment was a trifle on the long side. I found that if I turned up the collar and ran my bottom teeth up the inside of my mouth like Stewart Granger, I looked at least twenty. This worked every time. In fact on several occasions I even took other kids in with me.

If I could have afforded it, the cinema might have accounted for all of my leisure time, but economics do play a part in the life of a boy with only five bob a week pocket money. In fact I had another interest at the time: Charterhouse Boys' Club, which subsequently became a thirty-five-year obsession. This London mission-club, endowed by Charterhouse, the public school, existed for more than ninety years. During that time it made an enormous difference to the lives of thousands of people, young and old, who passed through its welcoming doors. In my own case, it was the greatest single institution in my life. At times it really was my entire life. I began associations and friendships in my first months at the club that I keep until this day.

For generations it bred continuity and security. My father had been a member when he was a child. This in effect made me something of a newcomer, because many families had ties that spanned three or even four generations. The 1960s and 1970s exodus from the inner cities finally destroyed the club's old format by taking away the continuity that had made it the social cornerstone of so many young lives. Not that Charterhouse school was alone in placing a mission in Southwark. Downside and

Wellington and the universities of Oxford and Cambridge all financed mission-clubs in the area. Each of these clubs generated loyalty among working-class boys that rivalled their national patriotism.

Girls were also catered for by the Charterhouse mission, but their building was further down the street, and except for weekend evenings the sexes were well segregated.

Not that the boys would have wished it any other way. With no feminine distractions, we could concentrate on the things that mattered most, which meant football, cricket, boxing, handball, hockey, snooker, billiards, table-tennis and occasionally, weekend camps in the Charterhouse school grounds at Godalming in Surrey.

For the price of one cinema admission, I could attend the club every evening of the week and play football or cricket at a distant park on Saturday afternoon. That was value indeed! In fact, if we could not afford the tram fares on Saturdays, the club would even pay that. Yet the economic aspect was irrelevant. It was the cameraderie that mattered.

Membership was broken down into 'houses' – Bodeites, Weekites, Hodgsonites and so on – like the school itself, which led to fierce competition. An inter-house handball match rarely finished without at least one stand-up fight between the competitors.

The club's greatest treasure was the gymnasium on the top floor. It no longer had a roof because a bomb had blown it off, but it could still be used for all of our ball games. A wild kick or over-zealous batting would send the ball soaring out through the charred rafters and across the rooftops.

A great sporting event was always the occasional excursion down to Godalming to play football against one of the Charterhouse school's many teams. My first such trip dispelled a myth, inherent among all working-class boys, that 'All posh kids are cissies'. I soon discovered that 'the cissies' were as determined as tanks, as hard as nails and very, very quick.

I was also impressed by the public schoolboys' living accommodation. Having seen countless Hollywood films featuring people from privileged backgrounds, we assumed that 'everyone' posh wore silk dressing-gowns, talked like Ronald Coleman and slept in their own warm, plush-carpeted bedrooms. We were therefore quite surprised to find that the dormitories for 'the posh kids' were slightly inferior to dog-kennels. There were few club boys who did not return from their first trip to Godalming without a six-inch bruise and a healthy new respect for their more privileged counterparts.

The whole business of growing up in the war was strange. It was the time between leaving school at fourteen and being conscripted into the services at eighteen. Together with new friends that I had made since joining the club, I decided that my four years were to be devoted to sport. A group of us played one game or another at every opportunity.

There was only one open space nearby big enough to pass as a football pitch, called Tabard Gardens. It is true that it was littered with obstructions such as shelter entrances, ventilator shafts and six-inch high concrete and steel emergency exits, yet the space was much in demand. Players would arise early on Sundays just to lay claim to it. Once a match had begun, then the two competing teams had the right of occupation until that match was finished. This made for some very long games indeed. In fact some unscrupulous teams would send their players home for dinner on a rota basis! The longest game I ever played in started at nine in the morning and did not finish until some twenty minutes after black-out time, around seven-thirty in the evening.

It was just after one of these marathon Sunday matches that I remembered I had yet to get myself another job. My employment with Miss Brock's sister, for which my parents had held such high hopes, had been a grave disappointment. I was really nothing more than an errand-boy. By December I could stand the monotony no longer and resigned. All my friends had dirty jobs and I envied them their scruffiness.

My mother had given me an ultimatum: 'Don't think that you are going to be a layabout for weeks and weeks. You get out and start yourself a new job next Monday or else!' It was seven o'clock on a Sunday evening and my ultimatum was due to expire the following morning, which also happened to be New Year's Day.

'You've cut it a bit fine, ain'tcha?' asked Georgie Blackwell, a team-mate and friend. 'I s'pose you could always come and work with Shortie and me at our firm. They're always needing people.'

George and his inseparable friend 'Shortie' Harper, worked together at the trade counter of W. H. Willcox and Co., a supplier of engineering parts and no more than fifteen minutes' walk away.

'Can you get dirty there?' I asked, ignoring George's backhanded compliment.

'Dirty? Yes, you can get really rotten if you want to.'

'All right, then, I'll come with you and see the manager in the morning.'

'Done!'

16. The initiation

At 7.45 on the biting cold New Year's morning of 1945 I called for George and, together with Shortie, the three of us made our way through the slushy streets to Willcox's. The firm had been in the borough for many years and my father had worked there briefly as a delivery boy when he first left school in 1918.

My interview with Mr Birch the manager was a farce. As long as I could tie string I could work in the dispatch department, doing nothing more stimulating than packing up parcels and boxes. Six men worked in this department, all of them either over military age or classified as unfit for military service. The manpower situation in such firms as Willcox's was really desperate.

'Because you are under sixteen, you can only work from eight in the morning until five in the afternoon, with three-quarters of an hour for dinner,' explained the manager reluctantly. 'We do not have a dinner-break on Saturdays because we finish early, at one o'clock, all right?'

It sounded an eternity to me. 'How much do I get?'

'Twenty-five shillings a week. You also get a free apron and use of the fire during your tea-break.' He gestured towards a small rounded cast-iron stove that stood smoking forlornly at the far end of the yard. It looked about as effective as a candle in the Yukon.

I instinctively turned up my nose.

'Well, how much d'you want, then?'

'I got thirty bob a week at my last job.'

'Okay,' he said without a second's hesitation, 'thirty bob it is, then. Can you start now?'

I was instantly furious with myself: I had the feeling that I could have stretched him to at least three quid without too much trouble.

By eight-thirty I had taken up my place at a work-bench and by eight-forty-five I had just about learnt the job. Four words kept rushing through my mind: 'This is a mistake! This is a mistake!'

'Here y'are, lad, this is an official issue,' smiled Joe Deadman, the pleasant-faced yard foreman. He handed me two tatty oil-stained sacks.

'What are they for?' I asked miserably.

'You wraps 'em around your feet. Keeps 'em nice 'n' warm.' He nodded his head cheerily as if he were some fairy queen who had just transported me into some palace of luxury.

Apart from my abject misery at the new job, I was also worried about my impending confession to my father. On the previous evening, when I had first mentioned my interest in employment at Willcox's, he had forbidden me contact with the firm. I had a feeling that his own departure from them had been anything but harmonious. If this was the case, how was I then to explain to him that not only had I begun work there but I hated it?

On reflection the answer was simple – I would lie. As far as he was concerned, I was going to be happier at Willcox's than I had ever been in my life. After all, it was entirely my fault that I now worked there. He had been so proud of me when I had begun in that office that I knew he must be feeling really let down now that I had left. All I had to do was to turn myself off mentally during working hours, and at Willcox's that was not difficult.

At this period of my life my need for Charterhouse Club was at its greatest. It filled the vacuum left by the frustrations of work. From the moment that I woke each morning until I entered the club building that evening, hardly anything else ever entered my mind. One of the main reasons for working at Willcox's had been the friendship of George and Shortie, yet other than on the journey to and from work I hardly ever saw them.

Then one day the monotony was broken when Mr Birch unexpectedly asked me, 'How would you like an afternoon off?'

'Me?' I pointed idiot-like to my own chest. 'Yeh, you bet! But when?' I stood quizzically, my finger still pointing, for a good thirty seconds after I had asked the question.

'This afternoon. Now, in fact. Of course it's not *really* an afternoon off. It's just that you'll be on loan to the 'wire-bound' department for a couple of hours or so. There's a fair bit of heavy lifting to do and, as you know, the wire-bound department is staffed almost entirely by women. I thought perhaps a strong young fellow like you may care to give them a bit of a hand. You don't mind do you?'

I suddenly looked at the manager in an entirely new light. His personality may not have been much but his psychology was superb. 'No, I don't mind at all.'

'Good!' He gave a satisfied nod. 'Report to the forelady when you arrive, she'll be expecting you.' He then gave a half smile and turned on his heels and left.

'You watch it,' snorted Dan, a humourless man whose workbench I shared. 'There's not a man in this yard who'll set foot in that wire-bound depot. D'you know that?'

I suddenly experienced a tiny quiver of doubt. 'Why, Dan? Why won't any man from this yard go round there? What's the matter with the place?'

'Well, you could try Beryl Frazer the forelady for a start.

135

She's nothing more than a camp commandant. "Bloody Beryl" her nickname is! She'll frighten the shits out of you, she will.'

'Now come on, Dan, tell me what's the matter with her.' I was now genuinely worried.

'What's the matter with her?' he echoed. 'She's like Hitler with tits, that's what she is, Hitler with tits!'

I laughed at his simile.

'You can laugh, you silly bastard, but she's even got his moustache!'

'The time for you to worry, young Ginger,' chimed in Joe Deadman, 'is when she shows up in his jock-strap!'

I looked quickly around at all of the chuckling faces and at first I was quite relieved. Then I saw Dan's face and I realized that he certainly wasn't joking.

'I don't know if you buggers are having me on or not. Anyway,' I chirruped, full of bravado, 'I ain't frightened of no woman, moustache or not.'

'Well you ought to be, son,' muttered Dan. 'You certainly ought to be.'

Deciding to ignore his warning, I turned up the collar of Uncle Sid's old overcoat, gave a Stewart Granger grimace of nonchalance and walked out into the now driving sleet.

Willcox's wire-bound depot was an antiquated building that was short on machinery and large on women, large being the operative word. Great heavy rubber hoses, many a foot or more thick, were placed on a lathe and turned while wire, emerging from coils through an aperture in the ceiling, was rolled around the hoses like cotton on a reel. Two women stood at each end of the hose, and while one used a lever to pull up the hose, her partner pulled it down in the same fashion.

The women in the wire-bound department had created an atmosphere of gaiety that would have made the walls collapse in our male-orientated warehouse. The first thing I noticed, even before I entered the building, was the noise. A radio blared out a stream of popular songs and the women accompanied most of them in a range of voices. The end of each song would be greeted by gales of giggles as there was always one singer who was at least half a verse behind.

The women all wore long tied green overalls and their hair was tightly turbaned. In spite of this all-embracing apparel, the sheer power of most of them vibrated through their drab outfits. Each looked capable of towing a ferry across the Volga. My warehouse bravado collapsed as I first laid eyes on these amazons. There was suddenly no doubt in my mind that I had been sent on some well-tried initiation ceremony. They did not need me for their 'heavy lifting'. Any one of them could have hoisted a hundredweight effortlessly.

'Ullo, cocky, what d' you want? Whatever it is, we've got it by the ton!'

I swung quickly around to see a stockily built woman of indeterminate age standing slightly behind me, a little to my left. She had obviously been dragging along a twelve-foot length of wire-bound hose, and one end of this huge hose still rested upon her ample left hip. Wisps of dark hair criss-crossed her top lip. She was not wearing the statutory overalls but light grey slacks and a dark-grey sweater. I knew her instantly: she was 'Bloody Beryl the forelady', alias 'Hitler with tits'!

'Well,' she persisted, 'what's the matter, cat got your tongue? I ain't got all bleedin' day, this is soddin' heavy. What d'you want?'

The hose had slipped down slightly, and to stop it moving further she flicked up her left hip and renewed her tight grasp upon its metal end. This sharp movement caused ripples to spread upwards and outwards from her hip like a brick in a pond. I remember wondering what happened to the ripples once they had reached the top of her right shoulder. Did they continue over and down her back, finally all meeting somewhere around her bum?

'Mister Birch sent me round. He said you needed someone to give you a hand . . . with some heavy lifting.' My voice fell to a whisper on the last four words.

'Ow, I see! Yer, yer, that's right, we do.' With surprising delicacy, she lowered the huge hose to the floor and turned to the dozen or so women who were within earshot. 'Girls! Girls!' she called. 'We've got a nice strong young man who's come round here to give us a bit of relief. 'Ow about that? Ennit nice?'

The oohs, ahs and ironic cheers that greeted that statement filled me with instant dismay.

'He'd 'ave to 'ave a good dinner down 'im first!' called out a very rounded redhead.

'Two minutes under me would be the death of 'im!' called another from deep in the group.

'Would it, Ginger-boy, would it?' asked Beryl of me.

'Er, would what?' I bleated, now very close to terror and fully realizing that I was vastly out of my depth.

'Two minutes under Vera, would it be the death of you?'

On the completion of that question, Vera emerged from the group. She was the most powerful lady in a room full of powerful ladies.

'Yeh, yeh, it would! It would! It most certainly would!' I fired out, panic-stricken.

'Yeh, I think so too,' agreed Beryl. 'Sorry, Vera, you're out of luck,' she called.

'Out of *what*?' responded Vera. Another great cheer from the women greeted Vera's answer.

'I said "luck", Vera, luck.' Beryl again turned to me.

'Bloody 'ell, Ginger-boy, you're gonna be a problem, you are. Any one o' these could eat you for tea!'

''Ow about Lil from the office? She's more 'is size. She's standin' 'ere as well.'

Amid cheers from her colleagues, a grinning Lil sidled to the front.

'Ginger-boy, by unanimous decision we're awarding you Lillian!' announced Beryl, as if she were bestowing upon me the heavyweight championship of the world.

My first impression of Lillian was that she was Humphrey Bogart in a frock. My second impression was that she was too old to be Bogart. The hair upon her top lip was even more impressive than Beryl's.

'Now then, Ginger-boy,' explained Beryl, 'if you're good, you can keep Lil. On the other 'and, if you're bad you can keep me, all right?'

I was now very close to tears. Suddenly I caught the eyes of two of the nearest of the overalled amazons and I could clearly see that they were twinkling merrily. I began to feel less afraid. It was obviously a leg-pull and I began to take heart.

'Come on, then, Ginger-boy, we ain't got all bleedin' day. There's a war on. We've got a lorry to load.'

By the door of the workshop lay a great pile of hose, neatly stacked and labelled and ready for transport. A young ATS girl was waiting patiently at the wheel of a lorry in the yard outside. Beryl began to fire out orders.

'We'll get a grip of these ends, Ginger-boy, 'cos the girls an' me like a good end, we do, an' just put your back under the middle section, all right?'

'All right,' I echoed.

It was soon clear to me that I had no real function to play in this loading process. Each quartet of women was more than competent to hoist the heavy sections of hose up on to the back of the vehicle. The purpose of my back being underneath the middle of these lengths was just to provide verbal ammunition for the women to fire.

'Oooh, 'e is strong, ain't 'e?'

'Come 'ere, Ginge, let's feel your muscles.'

'I could take 'im 'ome an' keep 'im in me bed like a teddy bear. 'Ow'd yer like to be me teddy bear, Ginge?'

Slowly the lorry filled and soon the last of the hose was swung aboard. I was by this time quite enjoying both the company and remarks of the women and I no longer felt intimidated by them. The driver signed Beryl's worksheet and the lorry reversed slowly out of the yard.

'Okay, girls!' called Beryl. 'Tea-time! D'you wanna cuppa before you go back, Ginger-boy?'

'Me? Oh, yeh, yes please!'

'Go an' 'ave a wash, then, Ginger, go on, off you go.'

'Wash?' I queried. Washes were extremely rare at Willcox's in wartime. In fact I had yet to find the basin in our warehouse.

'Of course wash! You don't think we're gonna sit down with you for tea, an' you not even washed proper!'

'But where?'

'Oh yeh, that's a point, I forgot that. We ain't got no gents 'ere. I'll tell you what, go in the ladies, no one'll mind. Go on, off you go.'

Beryl pointed to a small cream and green painted door at the far end of the workshop. I moved towards it reluctantly, not even noticing that very few of the girls were now in sight. Eventually I banged on the wooden door and twice called nervously, 'Is anyone in there?' Receiving no reply, I slid apprehensively inside. It was a sparse, whitewashed little room with two cubicles and one wash basin. A rusty pedal-bin stood forlornly in the corner. A small window had been boarded up after some exploded bomb. The only light came from a bare forty-watt bulb that hung dustily down from the centre of the ceiling. I crossed towards the wash basin but I had yet to touch it when the door opened and the fat redhead bounced cheerfully into the room.

''Ere!' she demanded with patently false indignation. 'What're you doin' 'ere?'

'I'm washing my hands, I was sent here by–'

'"I'm washing my hands",' she mimicked, cutting me short. 'Well, ain't we the gent, then? You must think I come down with the last shower of rain or something. Washin' your 'ands, indeed! 'Avin' a bleedin' good peep, more like it.' With that, she leaned back and popped her head out of the door and called loudly into the machine-room. ''Ere, gels! I've caught 'im, I've caught a peeper. Little Ginger's turned out to be a dirty little sod!'

The two cubicles opened together with suspicious speed and a couple of the amazing amazons stepped out. Not as much as the tape around their waists was displaced. Two more women joined the redhead at the door and in the distance I could hear Vera's dominant voice. I had most certainly walked into a trap, but for what purpose?

'Beryl's sent me in here, honest!' I pleaded. 'Why don't you ask her?'

'Beryl's 'ad to pop out for a minute or so,' announced Vera. 'So you'll 'ave to come up with a better story than that.'

'But it's true!' I insisted.

'Right, come on, gels!' sang out Vera. 'We'll just 'ave to give 'im the old wire-bound treatment. Trousers off!'

With the exception of the antiquated moustachioed Lillian, they were all very powerful ladies, yet they were more than a little surprised by the intensity of my kicks and struggles. Like all adolescent boys I had been looking forward to that first big occasion when my trousers would come off in some great romantic entanglement. Well, they were coming off all right now, but it wasn't what I had had in mind at all! Any assault by young *ladies* would have been quite bearable, after all, I could have made just a token resistance then given in like a gentleman. However, those half-dozen wire-bound battleaxes caused the terror to rise once again and with it destroy any tingle that I might have experienced in the loins.

My calls of alarm plus their cheers and giggles brought two more overalled tormentors running into the toilet. My struggles had by then exhausted me and, panting deeply, I gave up all resistance and waited anxiously for the next stage of the ritual.

Trousers, underpants, shoes and socks, all lay in an untidy heap on the cold stone floor, and I was left with a shirt and jersey.

'Okay, now lay 'im on the floor an' 'old 'im still a minute,' ordered the eager Vera as she disappeared out of the room.

No other discomfort of that scuffle matched the chill impact of that ice-cold floor upon my bare buttocks. The instant I touched it I yelled and arched my back up and away from it as if it had been red hot. Lillian soon solved this little problem for me by sitting herself down on my belly. The cold numbness of my buttocks soon spread and after a couple of minutes I found it to be almost tolerable.

''Ere we are, then,' announced Vera, holding a large jar in front of her as she strode gaily back into the toilet. 'Don't worry,' she added as she looked down at my apprehensive face, 'it's anointin' oil. Lift up 'is shirt, one of you.'

Lillian had my shirt up almost before Vera had finished speaking.

'Is that it, then?' asked Vera with mock incredulity. 'Is

that what 'e's been makin' all that bloody fuss about? I've seen better on a plate of whelks.'

'Don't you believe it,' countered the fat redhead. 'They're all like that at first but after a couple of minutes you can almost feed 'em buns.'

I made two instant decisions. First, I did not need anointing, and secondly no one was going to feed my willie with a bun! I lashed and kicked out once again and this time I almost slipped free. My struggles soon ceased, though, when the redhead joined Lillian on my stomach.

One merciful aspect of the position of these two women was that I could not actually see what Vera was now doing with the pot of bearing-grease. However I began most certainly to feel it. She smeared it everywhere: on to, around, underneath and in between; hills and hollows, cracks and crevices, all received a liberal covering.

Finally she stopped and climbed heavily to her feet. 'Okay, gels, just make sure 'e ain't got any grease on 'is shirt an' you can let 'im go.'

The fat woman and Lillian also stood up.

'Congratulations, Ginge, you've just 'ad a special wire-bound department christenin'. Ten selected ladies 'ave inspected you an' passed you fit for wear,' announced Vera as if she was awarding me a testimonial.

As I climbed to my feet one of the dragons handed me my clothes and I padded across the cold floor towards the wash basin. It was a little like leaving the dentist. One is always so brave *afterwards*. Well, I had just experienced my treatment and I now had nothing to worry about any more. Or so I thought.

''Allo, Ginger-boy, what's 'appened to your dickie, then?' I recognized the authoritative tones of Bloody Beryl instantly. 'I turn me back for just a minute an' this 'appens. Nice goin's-on, I must say.'

Now no longer caring, I turned and faced her. 'It's your bloody fault. Old Dan was right about you. "Hitler with tits" he called you and that's just what you are – a bloody camp commandant!'

'"Hitler with tits". Is that what he called me? I s'pose he calls me that because I nearly broke 'is arm when 'e tried to get 'em out. Vera reckons that that moaning old git was the only bloke who's ever failed the ceremony. Anyway – ' her voice softened appreciably, 'come into the kitchen an' I'll give you a clean-up.'

'No bloody fear! I'll do it myself, thanks.'

'Not 'ere, you won't. There's only cold water in 'ere. We'll 'ave to go in the kitchen an' boil a kettle. After an 'andful of washin' soda an' a drop o' turps you'll be as clean as a whistle in no time.'

Five minutes later I sat on a rickety old cane chair with a greasy sack wrapped around me and watched a reluctant-to-boil kettle.

It seemed that every male Willcox employee who had ever set foot in that department had received similar initiation. The 'girls', as Beryl somewhat misleadingly called them, did not mind a fellow making only token resistance, but their high moral scruples would apparently not permit active cooperation.

At last she poured the hot water from the kettle into a small washing-up bowl that stood in the old chipped sink. Producing a dubious grey rag from an old cupboard, she matched it with a bottle of turpentine substitute from another.

'Come on,' she said, tipping the bottle up on to the rag, 'I'll take the worst of it off with this.'

'Not on your life you –'

'Oh come on!' she interrupted. 'I'm an old hand at this, you know. I've washed more dicks in that chair . . .' She faded the rest of the sentence into a gale of laughter.

Half an hour or so later, I tiptoed stiffly back to the warehouse. It is difficult to walk with any degree of flexibility when your private parts have been assailed with turps and washing soda. That in itself would have been bad enough, but Beryl's hands had the texture of loose gravel.

As I limped into the despatch department, I was greeted by Dan who was weighing a wooden case he had just packed.

"'Ow'd you get on?' he asked eagerly. 'I bet they 'ad you, didn't they? I knew they would. Sex! That's all they think of round there. They get it out, did they? Held you down, I bet. 'Ow about that Beryl? She loves it, don't she? Can't keep her away, you know, flashin' her bloody tits everywhere. Hitler, she is, just like bloody Hitler!'

Over our meal that evening, I decided to broach the taboo subject of Willcox's with my father. I asked him if the wire-bound department was in existence during his days there, some twenty-seven years earlier.

'Yes,' he answered guardedly. 'It was, but it wasn't a place that a young boy would hang about in.'

'Why's that, dad?'

'Well, it was wartime, don't forget, and it was staffed almost entirely by women.'

'So?'

'Well, it just wasn't the right place to be in, that's all.'

'Did you ever go around there, dad?'

'Well, yes, but only the once.'

'What happened?'

'Er, I don't really remember. It was a very long time ago and I left the firm a day or so later.'

Dad would not be drawn again.

17. Win some, lose some

The news from the front became better each day. We had
not seen a German bomber for so many weeks that the
blackout regulations were eased. This, together with the
lighter spring nights and the gradual collapse of the
Germans, seemed to make every day much brighter. Then,
one sunny evening as we played football against Downside
boys' club, every boat in the Thames began to sound its
foghorn. 'It's over, boys, it's over! The war's all over!'
screeched a passing old lady as she struggled excitedly with
her mongrel's chain.

It was true, the war was finally over! For almost six years
we had lived with it; now it was finally at an end. But what
does one do when a war ends? There had been nothing in
the newspapers or on the radio to give us any guidance,
which was very unusual in wartime. We wondered if it was
covered by the rules but the referee said it wasn't. Some
players thought perhaps we should stop the game out of
respect. After much discussion, it was decided that the
match should take precedence over the peace and we
resumed play immediately. This was a great mistake.
Winning the war was one thing but losing three-nil to the
Catholics was serious.

That night a two-day holiday was announced on the
radio. Fourteen is of course a rotten age to celebrate the
end of a war. It is too old for a kid's party and too young
for emotions, or even to get drunk. We finally went to the

pictures to see Errol Flynn in *Virginia City*. All in all, I remember the end of the war as a tremendous anti-climax.

One way in which I did celebrate was to hand in my notice to Mr Birch. I had become totally disenchanted and dreaded each morning that I set out to work. It was in fact a good time to be looking for work – with demobilization not yet in full swing, there were vacancies in every trade and occupation. Given the opportunities available, it is difficult to explain my next choice of employment.

H. T. Cook was a city printer and stationers, secreted in a narrow alley not far from St Paul's. They had been searching for some weeks for 'an intelligent junior to learn a skilled trade' because an old skilled employee – a rulerer by profession – was slowly dying of tuberculosis. It was hoped that he could hold on long enough to train a successor before he finally keeled over and died. A rulerer, I discovered, was not a piece of straight wood but a skilled designer of high quality account books. The hours were long – 8 a.m. to 6 p.m. – but at least there was no Saturday work.

I soon came to the conclusion that being a rulerer's assistant was even more boring than being a packer. The work involved setting up a medieval-looking machine which consisted of an endless belt, a basin of ink and a dozen or so pens. The machine was so primitive that it was obviously dying along with the old craftsman. It was just a question of which would go first.

David Jackson produced account books that were miniature works of art. He was a round, slow-moving man who wheezed constantly. During our brief working time together he rarely stopped talking, not, however, to me but to the machines. 'Machines are like geraniums, you know,' he once panted. 'You have to talk to them to get the best out of them. It don't matter what your problem is, just as

147

long as you explain it to them they'll help you. Never fails!'

I liked Davie a lot, and under his guidance my pen-work improved rapidly. But I missed other company. All day long it was just Davie and me; even our tea-breaks were taken at our machine. On Thursday afternoons, Davie would send me to a nearby cafe for some bread pudding. Oh, how I loved this trip! I always took the long way round past St Paul's and fed my pleasure on the hundreds of different faces that I saw.

One morning as I climbed the last flight of stairs I heard no machine. I was surprised at this because Davie was always there before me, and besides, the light was on and the workshop door was partially open. Davie's sandwiches lay as usual on the window-sill, neatly wrapped in the previous day's newspaper, but of Davie himself there was no sign. I switched on the power and pressed the button to start up the machine. There was no response, it was totally dead. So too was Davie. He was wedged behind his beloved machine with the oil-can clutched firmly in his right hand.

The day after Davie died, the manager at Cook's sent for me and invited me to sit in his very comfortable chair. He swung it round to face a full-length mirror, then positioned himself behind me, slightly to the right.

'I suppose you are thinking of leaving us now, young man. Am I correct?'

I nodded.

'You are wondering how I knew. Again, correct?'

Once more I nodded.

'Well,' he said, placing two damp hands either side of my head, 'I'm a phrenologist. What do you think of that?'

I did not feel I could nod again because I had not the faintest idea what a phrenologist was.

'Your head's shape clearly indicates to me that you are

a born leader. I can see you – provided you have the correct guidance and stay at this firm – climbing high on the ladder of success. Now what you need to do is to go away and get down to some dedicated work and you will blossom.' He gave the chair a firm push and swung it around in a full circuit. 'Off you go and come back and see me in six months' time. I'll guarantee you will be astonished at your progress.'

I left that office elated, totally convinced that the whole of industry was just waiting for me and my head bumps. For weeks after that interview I would throw the word phrenology into any conversation I found myself engaged in.

Soon the Japanese surrender caused even more men to flood back on to the labour market. This surrender seemed somehow to coincide with a dramatic fall in the demand for really sensitive head-bumps. I handed in my notice and not a move was made to stop me.

Contrary to all our wartime hopes, the end of hostilities did not coincide with a return to peace and plenty. Food if anything became even scarcer. Yet someone always seemed able to provide a commodity that nobody else had seen for years. Occasionally it would be a banana; once I saw a grape! Even the boys' club had its sources. Bread and pineapple-chunk jam was our speciality. Heaven only knows where it came from, but on three evenings each week there it was – four slightly-stale loaves and a great label-less tin of allegedly 'pineapple-chunk jam'. I saw 'allegedly' because it tasted more of turnip than pineapple, and it was never sold by the slice, only by the sandwich – great thick sandwiches at that – so you could eat it without having to see it.

This feast was always absent on Saturdays, when the

whole atmosphere of the club changed. On Saturdays we were mixed. Just as soon as the girls entered the building, so the easy, relaxed tendency of the previous five days would stiffen. There was immediately segregation: the girls would take over the general-purpose room for their dancing (this they seemed quite happy to do with each other), while the boys gathered in the adjacent snooker-room. There, safe from the female presence, they would artificially relive the adventures, both real and imaginary, of their day's sport.

During the course of these evenings, slowly – oh, so slowly – the sexes would mix. It was not drink that loosened the tongues (the club was completely dry), it was the sheer frustration of seeing so many pretty girls and never really having the confidence to open a conversation. If it was winter, then ninety per cent of the boys' conversation was about football. If it was summer, then it would have been of cricket. Neither of these topics seemed to inspire in the girls the enraptured idolatry for which the boys longed.

One girl in particular the boys wished to impress. This was Annie, a slim, fair-haired girl in her mid-teens, who flowed like a sonnet. She had a superb figure and lovely hair which reached easily down to the small of her back. Annie's dresses had a figure-hugging tendency that followed every curve of her body down to her tapering waist; then the skirts would hang intriguingly in long swirling pleats that swung seductively at her every move.

When Annie walked she was sensational. When she danced she cleared the snooker-room of nattering footballers in something under four seconds. The great highlight of the evening would be Annie's jitterbug. This twisting, turning, gyrating dance would lift the hem of her dress well over waist high. The boys would then devote their whole attention to seeking 'the line'. The line was rather akin to a high tide-mark. Few of the girls owned stockings, most painted their legs to a line just above the knee. After all, no one was expected to see much above that. Annie, however, painted them much higher. All the way up, in fact. A swift glimpse of ice-blue knickers and a really high tide-mark was about as permissive as Saturday nights at Charterhouse club ever became. Most boys who had seen what Annie had to show slept that night with a sense of accomplishment.

Annie was considered to be as unobtainable as any Hollywood star. In retrospect, there was no reason for this; if anything she was far more of a conversationalist than the rest of the girls. Finally, after a year of this frustration, she appeared one night with a boy friend! One, furthermore, who neither played sport nor even talked about it! 'I reckon 'e's a poof,' was the general opinion. To us, Annie's new escort was complete anathema. He was the tallest person in the club, with a good suit and a large knot in his tie. He actually danced *and* conversed freely with all of the girls. In addition to this, he had the audacity to join the club! Oh how we hated him. We never spoke to him, of course, but that did not seem to bother him, and at the end of the evening he swept out with the adoring Annie on his muscular arm.

Eventually, as our teenage years slipped by, the barriers between the boys and the girls thawed. Almost fifty per cent of the boys married girls from the club, Annie being the first up the aisle. Four years of mixed weekend club-nights and only one premarital pregnancy says a great deal for our devotion to sport – or to the vicar's supervision.

Most of us club boys worked in local factories, with all of the mind-blowing boredom that factory life brings. Many of us dreamed that our way out would be through our sporting interests. We confided these fantasies only to our closest friends. I backed my dream two ways. First, I had been selected to play cricket for London Boys' Clubs against Birmingham; and then, after a trial with Crystal Palace Football Club, I joined them as a junior. The problem with the Palace was that it had some thirty juniors for just one side, so we were selected to play on alternate matches. It was during one of these weekends 'off', when I was able to play for Charterhouse that any serious chance of fulfilling my sporting ambitions finally disappeared.

That afternoon on Blackheath was a cutting-cold and rain-swept and our match had been under way for barely three minutes. My opponent pushed the ball past me and raced after it, a perfect situation in which to slide-tackle. As I dived feet-first across the muddy turf, I was aware that my right ankle had struck a divot of some kind and stopped sliding. The rest of my body, however, was eagerly following my left foot. My first thought was that my leg had disintegrated. Players two pitches away thought I had at least been disembowelled. In fact, other than a fair amount of puffiness over the top of the boot, there was not much to show for the scream I had emitted. As both teams assembled around me, I was given the standard treatment for every football injury except death: 'Rub it better and stand him up.' Each time they tried to stand me up, I promptly fell over again. So I was carried to the side of the pitch and play resumed. As the manager of the other team observed, 'These things always get better if left to themselves.' Well, by the end of the match it had not got better by itself, and eventually it was decided for each player to piggy-back me across the heath to the 53 bus-stop. Then there was a twenty-minute hike at the other end of the journey and the sixty-four stairs up to our flat.

'Would you like us to carry him around to Guy's Hospital, Mrs Cole?' asked Bill Hogan, our goalkeeper and by now my best friend.

'Not like that I wouldn't!' exclaimed mum. 'He's not going to that hospital until he's had a bath and changed his underclothes. How on earth did you get like that?' she said, turning her attention once more back to me.

'I only did one sliding tackle, ma,' I protested.

Exactly six hours after the injury had happened I was finally deposited, having bathed and changed, at the casualty department of Guy's Hospital. I had fractured my ankle and torn most of the ligaments.

The four weeks I spent on crutches and the surgeon's final verdict, 'No more sport for you, your ankle will always be a mess,' should have depressed me, yet somehow it never did. Serious football and cricket were now forever out of my reach – if indeed they had been within my capabilities in the first place – but I touched my first ball just two weeks after the injury, playing in goal in the club gym, with a plaster-cast and a walking stick.

18. Under canvas

Within a couple of days of leaving Cook's I began to work for Stuart Surridge, a sports suppliers and internationally known cricket-bat maker. There were two reasons for this choice. First, it was no more than three minutes' walk from home, and secondly – joy of joys – it was regularly visited by international cricketers. The work was as boring as all other factory work, but the companionship more than made up for it. For the first time since I had left school, I was working with youngsters of my own age.

Most of us were little more than operators of the antiquated and extremely dangerous machines. Strangely enough, accidents were almost unknown. That is, they were unknown until the day the insurance inspector arrived. On the strength of his carefully thought-out safety instructions, we had our first accident for years.

Part of my job was to trim the ends of the willow logs using a large circular saw. Usual practice was to wait until a dozen or so of these ends were cluttering up the bench then clear them by pulling one's fingertips along either side of the fast-revolving saw. It was, I suppose, a fairly risky manoeuvre, but considering some lads would actually sharpen pencils on the blade as it whizzed through its circuit, it was considered a relatively safe one.

My work-bench was just inside the main doors and therefore the first that the inspector saw during his tour of the factory. My fingertip clearing-action seemed to throw him into some kind of spluttering fit. All loose pieces must in future, he said, be removed by a specially designed push-tool. This was a rather grand name for what was little more than a stick, some eighteen inches long.

Under the close supervision of the inspector and now uncharacteristically helpful foreman, I tried out this revolutionary new safety practice. I found it particularly clumsy and said so. Putting down his brief-case with an exaggerated sigh, the visitor took up the push-tool and demonstrated how best to clear a cluttered saw-bench with perfect safety. Standing square on to the whirling blade, he reached forward with his push-tool but slightly misjudged the angle. Having now met the teeth of the saw face on, the recommended safety-tool rocketed back, arrow-like, in the direction from whence it came – straight through the hand of the puzzled inspector.

From that day on we seemed to average an accident a week. People took off fingertips, others crushed their toes, and the guv'nor entertained us right royally by falling down the sewer. But the real climax came the day before one summer holiday. It was a cracker! Four of us boys who contributed to it were going camping the following day and doubtless we *were* a little excited.

A large consignment of green willow logs needed to spend some weeks in the drying-kiln up on the fourth floor. The lift that carried all goods at Surridge's was an open-faced affair with no doors or brakes. It worked entirely by a series of pulleys, weights and manpower. A heavy load such as willow logs required the combined effort of three or four strapping young lads, all tugging together on the stout rope. 'Pull! . . . Pull! . . . Pull!' was a rallying cry that would echo up the shaft and throughout the whole building whenever a heavy load was being raised.

It was common practice to rest for a moment as the lift

reached each floor. However, just before we had begun, we had decided to attempt our personal record and reach the fourth floor in one quick burst. The main problem was that as our strength ebbed, so we began to be afflicted by the giggles, the slightest thing set us off. With just inches to go, the momentum of the lift had slowed almost to a standstill while we laughed like lunatics. Georgie Baker, the oldest of our group, had been the self-appointed caller, but his 'Pulls' had risen an octave after every giggle.

'Near . . . ly . . . there . . .' he panted. 'Pull . . . pull . . . pull as if you're pullin' the landlord off your mother!'

It was the final straw for me. I let go. The slow ascent of the lift stopped immediately. For a second the counterweight, which had almost reached ground level, didn't move. Then, imperceptibly at first, it slowly inched back upwards.

'Get . . . 'old . . . of the bleedin' . . . rope . . . yer . . . silly . . . b . . .' Exhaustion cut Georgie's words short.

'I . . . can't,' I whimpered, tears of helpless laughter streaming down my face.

There was nothing imperceptible about the rope now. It had begun to slip through the hands of my three companions with increasing speed. Each relinquished his hold at the same moment. The rope was by then a brown blur. The creaks, groans and rattles of the ancient roof-housed pulley-wheels could be heard all over the building. One brave soul ran towards us in an attempt to help, but if anyone had been rash enough to grab the rope they would have whistled up that lift-shaft just as quickly as that load was coming down.

'Look out!' yelled George as the bottom of the lift whizzed into sight.

For a split second we stared in total awe. We leapt back just before the old lift crashed on to its base. Willow logs exploded everywhere. The dust of a hundred years fell down that lift-shaft, billowing out into great choking clouds. Just as the last of the runaway logs slithered down the great heap and into the centre of the floor, there followed another great rumble. The wheel-housing was announcing its impending departure from the roof.

'Bloody 'ell!' exclaimed George, pursing his lips in a silent whistle and looking thoughtfully up the lift-shaft. 'Ole Surridge is goin' to 'ave the right needle with you.'

Just whether old Surridge did have the right needle with me, I never discovered. He was fortunately not in the factory that day, and the next we were off on holiday – and what a holiday.

Each August, Charterhouse Boys' Club leased a field for a week alongside an uninhabited stretch of road between Bembridge and Sandown on the Isle of Wight. I enjoyed this annual week so much that I used fondly to imagine being a millionaire and taking the entire Charterhouse Boys' Club camping, if not forever, then at least until the money ran out. I just assumed that we would all still be camping there in our eighties. After all, who in their right mind would wish to holiday anywhere else?

Each year, after travelling down from Waterloo and crossing on the ferry, we would catch the ancient local train from Ryde. At Bembridge, we would be met by 'old Tom', the local coal-merchant. This happy, imperturbable man would then transport the whole cheering camp and its luggage on the back of his prehistoric lorry. The word 'luggage' is something of a misnomer. Most lads took just one change of clothing which would still be unpacked when they returned home the following week. Also in their suitcases, though, would be a swimming costume, a towel and, for the exceptionally daring, a razor! With cold water and teenage acne, shaving was never a task for the fainthearted.

It was to be my third year away with the club and sadly my last for a while, because before next summer I would be called up for my national service. Most of my friends were in the same situation, so we were all determined to make it a memorable week. Well, memorable it certainly was, although for all of the wrong reasons. The preceding week had been an absolute scorcher – the Wednesday was the hottest day since 1870 – but the storms that began the day after we arrived continued, almost unabated, until we left for home the following Sunday. The unrelenting rain and the unseasonable temperatures provoked many other problems: summer insects in countless millions sought understandable refuge in our bell-tents. Within days we were smothered in deep bites, large lumps and frightening swellings. Then hygiene, never top of our priorities, practically disappeared. That row of washing bowls looked easily avoidable to any perishing young man whose entire wardrobe was geared for skin-blistering sunshine. Finally, a stomach upset – probably not too unrelated to hygiene – attacked everyone in the camp. At least it was a stomach upset to begin with. By the second day it was more akin to terminal dysentry.

In spite of these disasters, our spirits were as high as ever that week, and late on Wednesday afternoon, when the storms abated momentarily and for a brief moment a watery sun smudged the chill damp billowing clouds, we made our way down to the beach at nearby White Cliff Bay and hired two paddle-boats. George Baker and I shared one and Bill Hogan and Shortie Harper the other. The bay at White Cliff was surprisingly calm but I could see a line of choppy water out beyond the point and suggested we made for it. Bill and Shortie backed me up and George reluctantly agreed. It was the first wave we met that turned us over. Down and down we went. At first the water appeared a light green, then it began to darken. I was a non-swimmer at the time and a great panicker. George, on the other hand, had professed to be just as at home in the water as he was on land. True, his aversion to the stuff had thrown some doubt on this claim but we were not prepared for such an absence of buoyancy as he presented us with. I kicked and struggled and performed bubbling underwater screams before blessedly surfacing within a few inches of the upturned boat. George, however, had been thrown some six yards away. The manner in which he gained a handhold on that boat had nothing at all to do with swimming. He gained it simply by the sheer momentum of flaying his arms in the sea.

Thursday was the one day that Fred Seaman, the voluntary club leader and the camp's cook, shut shop. So we could either stay in camp and cook for ourselves, or go into one of the more accessible resorts and buy a meal. Shortie, George, Bill and me had been planning since last year to eat at our first 'posh restaurant'. The problem was that no one among our group had ever actually been in a posh restaurant – to eat or otherwise. While we all desperately wanted to go, we were apprehensive, to say the least. To this end we had cultivated the friendship of Frank Parrish, a senior member of the club who had recently left the army. Frank was in his mid-twenties and far more worldly-wise than anyone else we knew.

Under Frank's tutelage, ten of us had not only our first good wash of the week, but also a shave and a smear of Brylcreem. At 11.30 we stood outside the camp on the Bembridge Road waiting nervously for the Sandown bus.

Choosing a restaurant proved no easy task. There was always at least one of us whose nerve cracked just as we were about to enter. We would then hide our embarrassment by saying, 'Nah, I don't fancy this one much, let's look for another.' Finally Frank showed his irritation by pointing out that it was now nearly half-past one and even if everyone else disliked the next restaurant, then he (Frank) was going in alone. That did it. We needed Frank far more than he needed us and we followed like lambs as he led us to a ritzy place with table-cloths, carpets and wall-lights.

At first George was awestruck. He soon recovered to point out that it was the first cafe he had ever been in that did not have a spoon on a piece of string. Frank ordered soup, roast lamb, roast potatoes and peas. The rest of us did likewise. In fact we followed suit in everything that he did. I think if Frank had gone to the lavatory, then without as much as a thought each of us would have traipsed after him. We must have been the quietest group that restaurant ever had. Unless Frank spoke, no one did. That was, until George predictably broke the spell.

He had been experiencing a certain difficulty with a particularly stubborn piece of lamb. He had sawed determinedly at it with his knife, but this made no impression at all. He gritted his teeth and tried a slightly different angle. Presto! The knife zipped through the meat and catapulted a roast potato clear across the room and under the table of a family sitting on the far side. Before anyone could stop him he was off in eager pursuit. To the interest of the family, the consternation of the waiters, and the excruciating embarrassment of the rest of us, he not only appeared from under the table with the safely retrieved spud, but rubbed it on his jacket sleeve to remove some particularly tenacious carpet-pile! After he had rubbed it three or four times, he blew on it and then calmly slipped the whole thing into his mouth and sat down.

'Bloody 'ell,' he complained, opening his eyes wide and sucking in great gasps of air, 'that was 'ot!'

We each buried our faces almost in our gravy and desperately hid our eyes from one another. Shortie was the first to crack. He sprayed bits of half-chewed meat and potato all over me as he exploded into a fit of uncontrollable laughter. Within seconds, with the exception of our mentor, Frank Parrish, we were all in the same condition. Prudently Frank decided we should forego our afters, much to the relief of the waiting staff.

Fate had not yet finished with George for that day. The last bus of the evening deposited us wearily at our camp-site gates and we waved a cheery thank-you to the driver as he moved off towards Bembridge. We had crossed the road and were about to enter the site, when George let out a piercing yell: 'Bloody 'ell!! My old man's coat! It's on the bloody bus!' His father had lent him his new raincoat and a pair of shoes on condition that George guarded them with his life. George was away in a flash and our last sight of him was when he was a few yards from the rear of the bus, then they both disappeared fast around the bend. We waited for a moment or two but nothing happened so we continued on our way into the camp.

Thursday evenings round the camp-fires were always a favourite of mine. There, over the hot smoky tea, small groups would recount to each other their adventures of the day. We swopped our stories, then some two hours later fell wearily into bed. The fact that George had yet to put in an appearance had not unduly bothered anyone. It was well after midnight when we were rudely awoken by the blaspheming George stamping all over our sleeping bodies. He was neither quiet nor considerate as he trod on arms and legs with his frightening feet. He was beside himself with temper.

161

He had, he said, reached the bus soon after the first bend in the road. He had started to climb the old iron ladder that curved its way up the back of the vehicle to an open luggage-rack on the roof. But the driver – unaware of this drama – had at that moment accelerated fast out of the bend, an instant before George's feet had cleared the road. As his fingers closed tightly around the rungs, so the soles of his shoes peeled back, revealing the nails beneath. As a result of this escapade, George had found himself two miles from camp, with no money, no buses and not even able to walk in his shoes – shoes that he had been only reluctantly entrusted with in the first place and that now looked like old corned beef tins. George was not amused.

Friday morning it drizzled. Friday afternoon it rained. Friday night it poured. Saturday morning we had a storm. Saturday afternoon we had gales. Saturday night the tents blew down and on Sunday we came home. That last camp was a watershed for many of us. We were eighteen and soon off to the army. We had finally grown up. Well, almost.

19. Undefeated middleweight

'If you're warm you're in!' warned the fellow behind me at my national service medical.

If that had indeed been the case then we should all have failed; the place was absolutely freezing. As we filed slowly and nakedly past a desk, a spotty, unwholesome young man documented us and handed us each an identification slip, without even looking up. 'Report-to-the-doctor-at-the-end-of-the-hall,' he chanted. There a well-muffled figure wearing the statutory stethoscope sat huddled in a canvas chair.

'D'you play any sport?' he asked in a deep gruff voice. 'If so, what?'

'Er, cricket and football, sir.'

'Very well, bowl me a ball.'

'Pardon?'

'Bowl me a ball! Bowl me a ball!' he repeated irritably. 'If you play any sort of cricket you must know what "bowl me a ball" means, surely to God?'

'Well, yes,' I mumbled defensively, 'course I know what "bowl me a ball" means, but, well, where's the ball?'

'Imagine it, you fool! Imagine it! You don't think we're going to play cricket in here, do you? You in the nude and me in a chair? Just run up as if you were bowling a ball in a cricket match, that's all you have to do, simple isn't it?'

I bowled him a ball and a right idiot I felt too.

'Okay, next!' he called. 'D'you play any sport?'

I found myself wishing hard for a pole-vaulter.

'Cricket, sir.'

Our medical line-up had been drawn alphabetically and with no As or Bs in our batch, I had been the first in line. Everyone, it appeared, learnt from my experience. Before I had the chance to assess the bowling action of my successor, I was rapidly summoned into the next room. There a bored-looking individual peered solemnly into my ear, an even boreder one peeped up my bum. I assume they never saw each other because I was quickly passed on to the next white coat. There my genitals were roughly thrust aside with strict instructions to 'cough loudly'. I coughed. 'Louder!' I coughed louder and wondered what it was he could hear down there. I was in.

I had intimated at my interview that I was particularly keen to join the navy. I was told that was quite in order, all I needed to do was to sign on for five years. I said I wasn't that keen, what else was going? Perhaps I could join the air force? No, you can't join the air force, explained the interviewer, the air force doesn't like to be anyone's second choice. What else would you like? What else was there? According to my calculations, that only left the army. As they were now my *third* choice, I wondered how they would feel about it. Would they be slighted? No need to worry, said the interviewer, the army was nowhere near as touchy as the air force, they would take anyone.

'What regiment would you prefer? We like to give recruits a choice, it gives them a pride, y'know.'

'How about the Royal Fusiliers?' I offered. 'After all, they are a London regiment.'

'Do you have a second choice? You know, just in case?' he asked, his pen poised.

'Yes, Royal West Kents.'

'Excellent!' He nodded reassuringly. 'I see no problems there.'

Two weeks later I received the dreaded brown envelope. I was, it instructed, to report to Parson's Barracks, Aldershot, between 9 a.m. and 12 noon on Thursday, 9 December 1948, for service with the Royal Army Ordnance Corps. I had never even heard of them!

I decided to finish at Surridge's three days before I was to report to my unit. The Berlin airlift had gathered momentum and all the old soldiers at the factory had assured me we would soon be at war. I didn't fancy another war in the least, but if we were to have one there were at least six films that I would like to see first.

On 9 December, suitably broke, I enjoyed my last lie-in before catching the latest possible train for Aldershot. I arrived at the barracks with minutes to spare.

'You've cut it bleedin' fine, ain't you?' yelled a bristlingly smart drill sergeant, looking pointedly at the guardroom clock. 'Where'd you come from, China?'

'No, London.'

'London? London? London what?'

'Just London in – ' I paused while trying to think how to explain where London was situated. 'Well, London in London, I suppose.'

'D'you know what these things are, lad?' He screamed out the question as he pounded the stripes on his arm with three splayed fingers.

'Er, yeh, they're sergeant's stripes, I think.'

'Good, good,' he said sarcastically. 'So what am I, then?'

I had already come to a conclusion on that score. 'You're a sergeant, I suppose.'

'Very good indeed!' He beamed. 'You finally got it!' His mood changed and he bent forward intimidatingly, putting his face close to mine. 'An' don't you ever forget it, understand?'

I was fascinated by him. I had never seen anyone so sparkling; even his chin shone.

'Right! Get fell in. Quick march, one-two, one-two. Come on! Pick up the step!'

He marched stiffly and swiftly alongside me. In a futile effort to keep abreast with him, my ratio was three-steps-and-a-leap, three-steps-and-a-leap. I was moving, I felt, with all the elegance of a crippled camel.

We eventually reached the admin. unit, where I was handed over to another sergeant and documented. The first thing I noticed was that no one in the army ever talks to recruits, they bawl at them. Distance has nothing to do with it. A rookie is spoken to at the same volume whether he is two hundred yards away or nose-to-nose. The other obsession is numbers. Up until the moment I entered that barracks, I had never knowingly possessed a number in my life. Within minutes I not only had an eight-figure number that I could never remember, but I felt that the whole of Aldershot was busting to know it. I began to wonder if among all of the numbers allocated to our unit there was a particularly lucky one. I mean, was it a sort of mystery draw? Could that be the reason why so many people asked me for it? I had the feeling that if I recited '22091878' once more, someone would rush me before the commandant and claim a free holiday in the south of France.

From the admin. I was bustled along to the stores. There I moved slowly along the front of a long counter while an assortment of shifty-looking storemen piled mysterious articles of clothing and equipment high upon my outstretched arms. Each of them chorused out the particular article for which he was responsible as he thrust it on to the ever-growing pile in front of me.

'Boots – ankle!'

'Socks – worsted!'

'Drawers – woollen!'

'Housewife – for the use of.'

Housewife? What in heaven's name is a housewife? For a happy moment I wondered if we were going to be issued with some sort of plump surrogate mother to attend to all our daily needs. No such luck: it was just a small linen bag containing needles, cottons and darning wool. For all of the expertise that I could show with these, they might just as well have issued me with chop-sticks.

Parson's Barracks was just an assessment centre. For fourteen days we were taught to march, salute and remember our number. I became so neurotic about mine that I even had it on my toothbrush. The remainder of the time was filled with inoculations, vaccinations and aptitude tests.

In a moment of outrageous fantasy I had stated a preference to become a driver-mechanic. Anyone who knows me realizes that my mechanical ability is stretched by winding my watch. Nevertheless, together with a dozen or so other embryo mechanics, I sat a practical test. I was given the loose parts of a household light-fitting socket and instructed to reassemble it. An examiner watched me intently over his clipboard. After twenty minutes I indicated that I had finished. He slowly put down his board and carefully picked up the now-assembled socket. He tapped it lightly on the back of his hand and the whole thing disintegrated into more pieces than I had originally been handed. In total silence the examiner returned to his clipboard and drew a single straight line neatly through my name.

A week later I was ushered into the adjutant's office where a puzzled captain and a boyish second lieutenant sat gazing at my file.

'We do not see you as having any great aptitude for the Ordnance Corps, Cole. To that end, we are thinking of transferring you to some regiment where your gifts could be better utilized. Before I make this recommendation, I would like to ask you a personal question, d'you mind?'

'No, sir.'

'Do you keep a diary?'

'Yes, sir.'

'You do?' His face brightened. 'Since when?'

'Since I won one at the boys' club when I was fourteen, sir.'

'Excellent! You will no doubt be pleased to know that you will now be staying in the Corps, Cole.'

'I will, sir?'

'You will indeed, "sir". I'm sending you on a technical-clerk's course, beginning the first week after Christmas. We'll teach you to type.' He turned smugly to the second lieutenant. 'Amazing how many times that works, Daniel.'

After we had been in the army for precisely two weeks, the camp closed for Christmas and we were allocated seven days' leave! This passed all too quickly and two days before the end of the year, together with forty or so others, I reported to Salamanca Barracks on the other side of Aldershot. Parson's Barracks had been quite a civilized place, with its small, warm barrack-rooms and reasonable food. Salamanca Barracks, on the other hand, was as primitive as a swamp and about as inviting. The rooms were huge and high with next to no heating. Each morning the damp walls, both inside and out, were covered by ice.

My opinion of Salamanca was no doubt coloured by the two great mistakes I made there. The first was to make an official complaint about the food, and the second was to box for the unit.

It was common practice in the army for the orderly-officer and an accompanying sergeant to make the rounds of the mess-hall at mealtimes and enquire as to the quality of the fare. Our platoon had been on a snow-covered firing range all afternoon and we were freezing cold and hungry. As we queued outside the mess-hall in the swirling snow, the all-pervading aroma of freshly fried chips assailed our nostrils. We closed our eyes and tilted our heads like two dozen Bisto kids.

'Don't get too carried away,' called a disillusioned early diner. 'It's macaroni cheese with the chips.'

An immediate groan arose from the expectant queue. Macaroni cheese was *not* the chef's speciality.

'I'll swop anyone my macaroni cheese for their bread and jam,' I offered.

This trade-in was immediately taken up by the soldier in front of me and we completed the transaction the instant we were served.

Food at Salamanca was served on a specially designed tin tray which featured curves and hollows where the cook-house staff would drop in the appropriate course as the expectant diner filed past. With the evening meal there were always two slices of bread and a splodge of jam. *Always*, that is, except that night. That night no jam was on my tray, just a rather nasty stain where the jam had been.

'Er, excuse me, corp.' I gestured to the cookhouse corporal who stood at the end of the counter supervising events.

'Wassamatter with you, then?' he growled.

I tilted the tray in an effort to draw his attention to the absence of jam.

'That man's got *four* slices of bread!' he thundered.

169

Almost before I could move, a white-coated cookhouse assistant had snatched back two of the slices, needless to say the two *with* jam.

'But corp, I haven't got –'

'Will you bloody move along there? You're preventing these men from getting their meals.'

That was pure rabble-rousing and he knew it. An instant outbreak of hissing and booing broke out from the queue and it was all directed at me. I seethed at the injustice of the situation.

'I'm not having that,' I muttered, as I thrust my mug under the dribbling tea-urn. 'I'm going to complain to the orderly-officer.'

I soon demolished my chips, but had to wait a time-dragging fifteen minutes before the orderly-officer breezed in at the door. He strode briskly up to the end of each table.

'Any complaints?' He would already be moving on to the next table before his words had faded.

'Yessir!'

'What?'

'This man is complaining, SAH!' snapped the orderly-sergeant who was trailing a few feet behind.

'About what?'

'I don't know, SAH! What are you complaining to the orderly-officer about, lad?'

'The jam, sir. There isn't any.'

'This man claims he has no jam, SAH!'

The officer returned irritably to my table. 'What's the trouble with it? We get no more than that in the officers' mess, you know,' he reproved.

'But there isn't any jam, sir, just a stain,' I persisted.

'Take that man's name and number, sergeant, and look into it.'

'SAH!' crackled the sergeant.

The cookhouse corporal was looking daggers at me and I was already regretting my action. As the officer and his sergeant swept out of the hall, the corporal walked slowly and deliberately towards me.

'I knew it the instant I clapped eyes on you, laddie,' he snarled. 'I bet you're the sort who writes to his MP. Well, I'll not forget you, laddie, your card is marked!' With that he spun angrily on his heels and left.

I looked almost tearfully down at my two slices of now dry bread. What a fuss! And all over a spoonful of jam!

Days later, no doubt in an attempt to rekindle favour, I allowed my name to be put forward to box for the unit. It was to be a triangular match between three Aldershot district training camps. Of the eight scheduled fights, just one was supposed to be between two complete novices – me and my middleweight opponent from west London. The result of my selection was an immediate improvement in my food. Each mealtime the boxing team sat apart from everyone else and indulged themselves in some quite reasonable fare. In addition to this gastronomic treat, we were also promised a forty-eight-hour pass for the first weekend after the fights.

The actual day of the contest was a rest day for the fighters. Everyone else had been required to give blood. Although blood-donating was classified as voluntary, only the boxers escaped the needle and most of us spent the day dozing on our beds. When towards the end of the afternoon the donors began to filter back from the clinic, they fell somewhat pale-faced on to their beds. As the last of them entered the room, he was soon followed by the company sergeant-major.

'What are you men doing on your beds?' he boomed.

'We've just given blood, sir,' came back the chorus.

'Then get outside on the double and we'll make you up

some more! Move!' As each soldier leapt complainingly from the top of his blankets, I instinctively joined them.

'Oh no, not you, son,' murmured the CSM paternalistically. 'You carry on lying there and have a good rest – you're boxing tonight.'

I could barely take it in! A sergeant-major who didn't shout? And he was talking to me! That settled it. I was determined now to win for the company. After a few kind words from the sergeant-major, I would have taken on the world champion.

Mine was the last but one contest of the evening. My trainer, lance-corporal Chalky White, had convinced me that I could not lose.

'You box right-handed but you're naturally left-handed. Do you know what that means?' I confessed I did not. 'It means that your left is naturally lethal, it'll never be out of his face! He's a novice just like you, so just keep pushing out that left and it'll be a formality.'

The referee had a quick word with us and the bell clanged. All I had to do now was throw out that old lightning left. I threw it out. He ducked, weaved and held my extended fist under his left arm and knocked the absolute daylights out of me. The referee immediately stopped the fight and cautioned him, but the damage was already done. I had been conned. The bloke was no novice, he was a street better than me – and he hurt! Blows rained on me from all angles and I have never felt so helpless in my life.

Finally, after what seemed a good hour, the bell sounded. I have never been so pleased just to sit down! Absolutely every part of me ached, even my knees, and they had been one of the few places that he hadn't yet hit.

'You're doin' great, Ginge lad!' exclaimed Chalky enthusiastically. 'Really great. Keep that ole left goin' an' you'll worry 'im sick!'

If I knew little about the first round, the second was just a blur. I honestly expected – and hoped – that the referee would stop it at any moment. I had two cuts inside my mouth, my lips felt like cushions and I had a tremendous urge to lie down and be sick. The referee came over to my corner during the second interval to ask if I was okay. I was too tired to answer.

'He's fine, ref, he's fine,' assured Chalky. 'He's got terrific stamina.'

'You sure? He don't look too fine to me. What round is coming up, son?' he asked.

I took a couple of deep breaths and finally blurted out, 'Th . . . re . . . e.'

'Very well, but I'll be watching closely,' he said to Chalky.

As we approached each other at the start of the last round, the very first punch he threw caught me under the left ear. The pain was incredible, it was as if a nail had been driven in. I lashed out in blind fury and felt a terrible thud on the end of my fist. My wrist now ached as much as the rest of me. I brushed the sweat from my eyes and realized that my opponent was now sitting on the floor. Could I kick him, I wondered? It seemed the referee had read my mind. Taking me roughly by my shoulder, he pushed me into a corner. He then had a quiet word with my opponent, who had by now climbed to his feet. Seemingly satisfied, he nodded and quickly brushed the gloves. 'Box on!' he commanded.

I have never hated anyone like I hated that bloke. I rushed at him, but I doubt if I even hit him, I think I just ran him over. Whatever I did, he went down again. The rest of the round consisted of me charging about all over the ring and not hitting anything much. To my relief I was still on my feet when the final bell sounded.

'Green is the winner!' said the announcement a few moments later.

Well, I did not begrudge him his win. He was obviously a far better boxer than me and I had decided from round one that this was to be my one and only fight. All I wanted was to get out of that ring.

'Congratulations,' said my opponent with a wry shake of the head.

'Great stuff, Ginger boy!' thumped Chalky excitedly on to my back.

'Good fight, son,' said the referee.

'Here, hang on,' I gasped bewildered at Chalky. 'Who's won this bloody fight?'

'You 'ave, of course!'

'But my name's not Green!'

'No, but your bleedin' vest is! They don't give you the fight by your name, they give it you by your corner – an' you're in the green corner. You've won!'

'That's the bentest decision I've ever known! He slaughtered me! He's covered in blood and it's all mine!' I was terrified in case I was required to fight again. I knew I had a better chance of escaping if I had lost.

'I've never met anyone like you,' said the puzzled Chalky. 'Anyone'd think you didn't want to win.'

'I don't mind winning, Chalky, I just don't like fighting!'

My initial reaction was later confirmed to me as I sat opposite my opponent at the customary steak-and-chip dinner. I winced at every mouthful as the salt and vinegar sought out the abrasions around my lips and gums. I felt as if I had been hit by a truck, and he was totally unmarked! If this, then, was winning, there was no way that I was going to stay around long enough to lose. I decided to end my short boxing career undefeated. Boxing, I concluded, was a mug's game.

I stared intently into the mirror next morning. I was worried that my split lips and black eye would not clear up in time for my weekend pass. I had shed blood for that weekend – lots of it – and I did not want it marred by two great thick lips. That day the boxing team discovered what everyone else had known for weeks. The weekend leave was not to be the sole prerogative of the boxers. Subject to an inspection, every recruit in the camp was to receive a forty-eight-hour pass, whether he had fought or not.

On Friday afternoon, ninety-six excited recruits caught the London-bound train from Aldershot. There should have been ninety-seven but the orderly-officer reckoned I had a dirty rifle. It looked so bad in some places, he claimed, that it could have had jam on it.

By early spring we had completed our basic training. For three months we had marched, shot and typed. According to army records, I was not only a first-class soldier but a first-class typist too. I made them wrong on both counts.

After two weeks' embarkation leave, we were told, we were all to be posted to Germany. The camp-padre wasted no time in warning us of the wanton ways of German women and the evil things they would do for a few cigarettes. It was quite impressive. The next morning we all set off on leave, each man with the sole intention of buying as many fags as he could lay his grubby little hands on.

20. Max Miller and a first date

It was around this period that a confusion arose in my neatly programmed sporting life. I had been to a party and met an attractive young girl who began to take up more and more of my leave times. This was a most unfortunate complication, the reason being twofold. First, my leaves were never long enough to share with both a girl *and* the club. Secondly, and this really was a heresy, Joan was not a club member! I was soon going to Germany for at least fifteen months, I therefore hoped the problem would resolve itself without me even having to make a decision. However, the fact that our relationship survived its potentially disastrous first date, should have given some indication of its endurance.

On that evening, in an effort to impress with my sophistication, I had decided to avoid the cinema. I mean, absolutely every couple I knew went to the cinema for their first date. I was going to be different. We would go to the theatre! Mrs Pudsey, a neighbour of ours, was a cleaner at the New Cross Empire and had constantly bragged of her ability to acquire tickets at greatly reduced prices. Well, two five-bob seats for six shillings were not to be lightly dismissed. As a result, Joan and I stepped off the tram just in time for the second house. In my eagerness to impress, I had not noticed who was appearing. As we stepped off the tram I glanced quizzically up at the theatre lights. Within seconds I had closed my eyes in total dismay.

The New Cross Empire Proudly Presents
The Cheeky Chappie Himself!
The One and Only Max Miller

Now Max was great, many would say the greatest, but whatever Max would be on a Saturday night at the New Cross Empire, he most certainly would not be *romantic*. Fingers crossed, I led Joan to our excellent seats in the circle. Mrs Pudsey had indeed done us proud. The first half of the show was the usual hotch-potch of singers, jugglers and dancers. All were excellent in their way but the Saturday night audience could scarcely hide its impatience until the great man himself appeared. Finally the tinny pit-orchestra struck up the opening bars of 'Mary from the Dairy'. To storming cheers of expectancy, Max strode on to the stage in his white hat and ridiculous suit. Great play was made of Maxie's vulgarity and his obscene stories. His punctuations, pauses, innuendoes, double-entendres and, above all, his incredibly saucy blue eyes looking cheekily up to the gods soon had the audience rolling in the aisles. Well, perhaps not quite *all* the audience. There were just two who sat stony-faced, pretending they had no idea at all what the sod was on about.

Since surviving that very first date, we had seen a great deal of each other. Then, on a cold damp Wednesday at Waterloo, we were scheduled to say our last goodbye for over a year. My posting to Germany was going to be a real test, particularly with two hundred cigarettes stowed secretly away in the bottom of my kit-bag.

Within ninety minutes of leaving Waterloo, I was back in the gloom of Salamanca Barracks. Early next morning the whole unit set off for the RAOC transit camp at Feltham in Middlesex, a spring-board to RAOC depots all over the world. At last we held our final parade at Feltham and, soon after, ninety-seven whistling men marched out of the camp gates and down the half mile of High Street to the railway station. As the train rolled into the station, the men broke ranks and scrambled to share a compartment with their friends. Two sergeants ran up and down the platform, pushing the heavily laden troops through the narrow doors.

The carriage-door slammed shut and I suddenly realized that I was unable to move my left hand. I glanced almost casually to see the cause of this restraint. To my horror I saw that my fingertips had disappeared into the crack of the closed door! The strange thing was, there was no pain. At least there wasn't until I frantically opened the door with my other hand. Then I felt as though my fingers had been crushed between a hundred red-hot needles. My last recollections were of pain, screams and a red-faced major.

Some minutes later I came to. I lay on my back blinking into the bright sunshine. The train had disappeared, together with every army friend I had. The two sergeants stared anxiously down at me and the fat major was slapping my face and chanting repetitively, 'You-did-it-on-purpose-didn't-you? You-did-it-on-purpose-didn't-you?' Although still confused, I was conscious enough to realize there was nothing I could do about the pain from my fingers. I could, however, do something about the crouching idiot who was smacking my face. Before I could regain a total composure, I instinctively struck out with my right fist and screamed, 'No-I-didn't! No-I-didn't!' The two sergeants instantly dived on me, while the fat major recoiled with a bloodied mouth. I was by this time quite rational and looked with more horror at the major's split lip than I did at my own crushed fingers.

'Close arrest! Close arrest! That man is under close

arrest, sergeant. Get him up!'

By this time the pain from my fingers was causing my mouth to twitch. In addition, the substantial breakfast I had eaten two hours earlier was becoming restless. Before either sergeant had time to react, I gave a spasmic jerk and vomited, straight over the major's feet. It seemed to be an appropriate time to faint again. So I did. I remember feeling quite surprised how easy it was. I just closed my eyes and off I went.

An ambulance arrived and returned the four of us to the transit camp. There the medical officer injected me with morphine and arranged a transfer to Millbank military hospital, some twelve miles away in central London.

The sixteen days I was to spend in that hospital was one of the best holidays of my life. It is compulsory in service hospitals for patients to contribute to the maintenance of the ward, by scrubbing, cleaning, cooking and polishing. Just three days after a stomach operation, for example, I saw a ward-mate crouching down polishing the floor. On the other hand, poor soldiers with injured hands can do very few of these chores. They are usually given a four-hour pass, just to get them out of the way.

These four-hour passes were the golden key to bliss. The white shirt and red tie that every uniformed soldier was required to wear while a hospital patient enabled most squaddies to enter West End cinemas free of charge. This was never an official policy but an approach to the pay-box would guarantee a kindly attendant escorting you straight into the auditorium. It was the 'poor wounded soldier' syndrome. For me to have found myself housed for two weeks within twenty minutes' walk of most West End cinemas, with free admission to the best seats in the house, was quite simply paradise.

There was, however, an embarrassing little problem

with friends and neighbours. Everyone had made their long sad goodbyes, not expecting to see me again for at least twelve months. Yet there I was, so close to home that I could – and did – pop back for tea! Then there was Joan. I courageously met her outside Mayfair telephone exchange where she worked, just days after she had tearfully told her sympathetic friends that I was gone for a year.

However, I manfully adjusted and within a week was playing football for the club again, albeit with a well-bandaged hand. Although my fingers were making steady progress, I rekindled my old ankle injury in a particularly brawling cup-tie. The ward doctor, when he discovered that I had sprained an ankle playing football just a week after he had diagnosed that I was too ill to return to the army, despatched me back to Feltham with instructions that I was to report to Millbank daily as an outpatient. Sadly, outpatients were required to return their white shirt and red tie. My two weeks in a cinematic utopia were therefore at an end.

That smack in the mouth that I had inflicted on the fat major had been put down to shock and I was officially informed that no proceedings were to be taken against me. It had not been forgotten, however, and after a patient three-month wait he achieved a sweet revenge. It was a 7 a.m. parade and as the corporal stood reading out the day's fatigues, the fat major stood hovering in the background. Just before the squad moved off to their tasks, he called the men once more to order.

'I want two volunteers!' he bellowed.

Now although it is a strict army tradition to volunteer for nothing, I somehow had a gut feeling about this one. I took one pace forward.

'Anyone else?' he roared. 'I want one more volunteer.'

No one moved for almost a minute, then two Scots lads in the front row took faltering steps forward.

'That's three of you and I only need two.' He nodded almost imperceptibly. 'Very well, fall out you two and get your kit. You'll be leaving this afternoon.'

'Er, where to, sir?' asked the braver of the pair.

'British embassy in Washington,' he grunted. 'Cut along now, you've not much time.'

I closed my eyes in disappointment.

'Incidentally, Cole,' he continued, 'when are you due for a discharge from your hospital treatment?'

'Er, yesterday, sir.'

'Good, you can also fall out and get your kit.'

I felt my face stupidly light up. 'Washington, sir?'

'No, Germany, "sir", you're on the noon draft. Or you will be if you can keep your hands out of door-cracks.'

'Sir,' I acknowledged, sighing at my own gullibility.

For the first time since I had punched his face, I looked him straight in the eye. I could not actually swear to it but I believe I may have caught just the hint of a smile.

21. Joining the other side?

For the next fourteen months my home was Pinewood Camp on the north German plain, some thirty miles from Minden. I soon forgot the padre's warning and parted with my cigarettes – unfortunately in a card game. National service had been cut from two years to eighteen months and slowly my demobilization date crept closer. Finally, in June 1950, I was returned to Aldershot, whence it all began, and released once more into civilian life. Then, as the North Korean tanks rolled into South Korea, demobilization was at first suspended, then national service reverted to being two years. I had avoided that little set-back by just twelve days.

It was during my demobilization leave that Joan and I decided to become engaged. I had always promised that I would take employment seriously once national service was behind me: with the prospect of marriage within two years, I had to keep that promise. 'A trade, that's what you need, lad, a trade,' I was told by all and sundry. That was all very well but what trade? In total confusion, I attended a Ministry of Labour advice centre. There I was told of a trade that I could learn and then perform anywhere in the country, or perhaps even the world.

'There'll always be a call for it – always has been, always will be!'

'Stonemasonry? But I thought convicts did that!' I protested.

'Highly skilled trade, son,' said the clerk reprovingly. 'You attend a government training centre for six months, then serve a further eighteen months with an employer. You'll learn as much in that time as you would in an eternity as an apprentice. Five years' time, son, you'll be building your own cathedral, you'll see.'

Well, I never did build my own cathedral, although I worked on the Royal Festival Hall and the Air Force Memorial at Runnymede. I impressed the family with a small stone memorial to my grandfather soon after he died; but they would have been even more impressed if it had not split in two at the very first frost.

At the training centre in Middlesex there were few formalities or introductions. I entered the place at eight-thirty and by nine o'clock I was whacking my first piece of stone. By ten o'clock I had my first blister. I finished my course in early January 1951 and was soon fixed up at Holloways, a large, bleak stoneyard alongside the Battersea railway sidings. It had a high roof to keep out the rain but no sides, 'to enable the stone dust to blow away', I was told. The Siberian winds that began on the Russian plains had whipped themselves to a fine old frenzy by the time they reached Battersea. Whatever dust did not whirl out of that yard whirled instead into the eyes of anyone daft enough to be looking up. One old mason was the yard specialist in removing stone fragments from eyes. His procedure was to pull back the eyelid and sweep underneath it with long coiled horse-hairs. Blinding tears would follow but soon afterwards he would present the victim with the offending fragment with all the panache of a bullet-retrieving surgeon.

In an effort to stave off the cold of this offending wind, four coke-braziers were scattered throughout the yard with just a half-hundredweight of coke between them. In order to preserve every last vestige of cinder, the fire was never allowed to burn out completely. Just as it began to die down and the heat faded, it was extinguished in the most unorthodox fashion. The nearest mason would put down his mallet, shuffle over to the fire and lift his apron. He would then part his coat, unbutton his trousers and studiously urinate on the dying embers. The angry hiss of steam would be heard all over the yard, as one by one the braziers were doused. Billowing clouds of vapour would roll up to the roof and the stench would be appalling!

The yard was extremely busy. The Festival of Britain was due to begin on 3 May and the Festival Hall was to be the permanent centrepiece of the whole display. Overtime was in abundance. I was saving hard for my marriage and frequently worked eleven hours a day. In spite of this frenzy of activity, a feeling of impending gloom hung over the whole trade. Building with stone was simply too expensive. Concrete and glass were replacing it rapidly. By midsummer overtime had vanished. There was still work to be had on the memorial (a really beautiful building) but many of the twenty-five masons in the yard were looking around for another employer. This winding-down process gathered momentum until there were just half a dozen masons and the trainees and apprentices remaining.

In the meantime Joan had found us a flat! Her method was slightly unorthodox. In her work as a telephone operator she had reconnected a caller who had lost her twopence in the box. While listening to make sure that on the second attempt the caller had a good connection, Joan realized that the purpose of the call was to offer an agency a flat for rent in the Brixton area. Unfurnished flats were like gold-dust at that time, and most newly-weds lived with one or other of their parents. We were both determined to avoid doing this. So the instant the caller rang off, Joan dialled the agency herself and asked casually if there just happened to be any unfurnished flats for rent in the vicinity of Brixton. 'That's truly remarkable!' exclaimed the amazed agent. 'Would you believe that for the first time since the war, one has come in? And barely ten seconds ago!' Within two weeks we had paid one year's rent in advance (thirty shillings a week) and taken on the tenancy. It was a tiny, damp basement in an appalling state of repair. Situated immediately above the northern underground line, it vibrated like Vesuvius every time a train passed through. But at least it meant we could now plan a wedding.

I was football-secretary at the time and my first task was to ensure that we did not have a match on the chosen day. I knew that unless we had a match-free Saturday, I would be lucky to obtain a best man, never mind a congregation. The league authorities were not too impressed, but after my pledge to cut short my honeymoon to play a cup-tie, they relented. I decided to keep this from Joan.

The real highlight of our wedding day was to be the party in the evening. All of the family were looking forward to it – we had not had a good family party since pre-war days. The reception was held above a pub near the Elephant and Castle and a three-man band was engaged for three hours for three pounds. The party was certainly living up to all our expectations when Joan and I left for our honeymoon at nine-thirty that evening (we were to stay at her sister's house in Bournemouth). Soon after, though, matters apparently got a little out of hand. My grandmother, who had officiated so well as matriarch at the boisterous pre-war do's, was now well into her seventies and eaten up with rheumatism. With the sad demise of my grandfather, there was no one else to see fair play. At ten-thirty the first drink hurtled across the room. It was soon followed by an aunt,

185

two uncles and a window. No one was sure how best to quell the brawl. My mother-in-law, in the absence of any alternative plan, gave the band thirty-bob to play longer and louder. That, plus the arrival of the police van, seemed to do the trick. At least, the members of my football team all assured me on my return that it was the best party they had ever been to.

At five-thirty on the last morning of our honeymoon, I woke Joan – not without some difficulty – in order to catch the first train back to London. Twelve hours later we had beaten Stairway 5–1 in the first round of the cup. A wedding; a party; a 5–1 cup-tie win. All-in-all I considered it to have been a pretty successful week.

After those dizzy heights reality soon descended.

The day before my wedding, the foreman at the stoneyard had asked me my long-term plans.

I shrugged. 'Other than finishing my training, I haven't really got any.'

'Well get some!' he retorted. 'You'll never be a mason as long as you've got a hole in your arse. I've only kept you on because you're getting married. I give this place three months at the outside, then it'll close, together with most of the other yards in London. Do yourself a favour, Ginger-boy, get out of it. The trade's no good, it's finished!'

I knew he was right, of course, although I had been shutting my eyes to the fact. I returned to work on the Monday after our honeymoon to find everyone in the yard just marking time.

'What do you think you should try next?' asked Joan as we discussed the matter over tea the following Saturday.

'I was half thinking of trying the police force, but I think my education, or rather lack of it, will be the stumbling block. Perhaps I'll try the buses?' I answered without enthusiasm.

I turned my gaze to the football results in the evening paper. There, as if by magic, was an advertisement for the police.

'What d'you reckon?' I asked, expecting her to be totally opposed to the thought.

'I think it's a good idea. I rather fancy the thought of being married to a policeman.'

'I should think old Lynnie would also be pleased, if he's still alive.'

'Who's "old Lynnie"?'

'He was my last teacher. It would help him even up the balance of our old class. At the last count we had two street-bookmakers, two rag-and-bone merchants, a confidence trickster and one lad serving life-imprisonment for murder because he was too young to hang. And now, he might even have a copper! I wonder what's worst?'

'I should think he'll be very pleased,' she announced loyally.

'*He* might be pleased but I'm sure *they* won't,' I muttered. 'Most of them will think I've joined the other side. And God only knows what my grandfather would have made of it. He would probably compare it to going over to the Germans. I bet he'll turn in his grave if they accept me.'

'I shouldn't think so,' she smiled. 'Knowing your grandfather, he'd probably just ask you for bail.'

I thought she had a strong point there and instantly felt better.

Within two weeks I received acknowledgement of my application and a month later I reported for a medical. I was then requested to return the following week for a written exam and final interview. I was a little worried about this exam. On the credit side, I was quite good on current affairs and interviews seldom bothered me. I could draw a pretty fair map of the Normandy landings and recognize every Allied aircraft of World War Two. In addition I knew every England football team since 1945 and every Errol Flynn picture since the same period. On the debit side, that was all I knew and I could not see what possible use it was to the police.

The set test was the old civil service third-class entrance exam, in which it was possible to skip subjects about which one knew nothing – in my case maths – and instead concentrate on happier themes. In this way one could answer enough questions to slip through the net. We sat the written examination in the morning and were told the results first thing after lunch, enabling the successful ones to prepare themselves for their interview and the losers to adjourn to the pub.

Having scraped through the written test, I was the last applicant of the afternoon to receive an interview. I was shepherded into a room and shown to a chair that faced four very senior-looking police officers. They began to ask the usual predictable questions, ranging from why was I joining, to what newspaper I read, so I gave the usual predictable answers. This seemed to satisfy them and soon the questions lapsed. They looked self-consciously at each other before the one who appeared to have the senior rank thanked me for my time and nodded towards the door. Suitably dismissed, I made swift tracks for home.

Joan asked me more questions on my return than the panel had during the whole of the interview. I was unable to answer most of them but a few days later, just before I left for work, an envelope arrived that answered most of them for me. It stated that I was to report to the

Metropolitan Police Training School on Monday, 1 December 1952.

I was instantly full of doubt. 'I'm not sure I want to go now,' I mumbled nervously to Joan.

'Why ever not?' she asked in genuine surprise.

'Well, other than that interview, I've not so much as spoken to a copper in my life. I've been spoken to *by* them a few times but I don't think that counts. To be perfectly honest, well, I just don't think that it's me.'

Full of indecision, I cycled the four miles to work and parked my cycle in the rack. It was a damp, dreary November day and as I walked down the empty yard a persistent mist clung ghost-like to the railway sidings. The scattered stone slabs made it look like a Dickensian churchyard. I glanced up to the office at the end of the yard. There, under a green-shaded light, I could see the foreman studying the day's racing programme. 'Is this it?' I thought. 'Is this my entire future? A chill barren stoneyard – and only that if I am lucky. What happens if I am unlucky?' I suppose I made the decision without even thinking about the implications. I walked swiftly into the dusty office.

'Dave, I'm leaving.'

'When?' he asked, without even lifting his gaze.

'End of the week, all right?'

He said nothing at first, then folded his paper with slow deliberation. 'What are you going to do, join the police?'

'That's right!' I exclaimed incredulously. 'But how d'you know?'

'It's what I would have done if I'd been you. The trade's dead. Besides,' he broke off and looked closely at me for a moment. A slight smile played around his mouth. 'All coppers are bastards, they say. Perhaps you're just finding your own level. Quite frankly, Ginger-boy, you may as well go now – this minute. There's no work coming in at all and

I should think we'll close down totally within a month. Anyway, best of luck.' He held out his hand.

It was as simple and as quick as that. At a quarter to eight I had set out for work. At a quarter to nine I was home again, having given up a trade. I sat in the armchair with a cup of tea and attempted to sort out my thoughts. Had I really joined the other side? 'All coppers are bastards,' the foreman had said. Would I make a better bastard than I did a stonemason? I supposed I would have to. I had just sold all my tools.

Fontana Paperbacks: Non-fiction

Fontana is a leading paperback publisher of non-fiction. Below are some recent titles.

- ☐ POLICEMAN'S LOT Harry Cole £2.95
- ☐ POLICEMAN'S PATROL Harry Cole £2.95
- ☐ POLICEMAN'S PROGRESS Harry Cole £2.95
- ☐ POLICEMAN'S PRELUDE Harry Cole £2.95
- ☐ POLICEMAN'S STORY Harry Cole £2.95
- ☐ POLICEMAN'S PATCH Harry Cole £2.95
- ☐ POLICEMAN'S GAZETTE Harry Cole £2.95
- ☐ VET FOR ALL SEASONS Hugh Lasgarn £2.95
- ☐ IMPRESSIONS OF MY LIFE Mike Yarwood £2.95
- ☐ ROYAL HAUNTINGS Joan Forman £3.50
- ☐ A GRAIN OF TRUTH Jack Webster £2.95
- ☐ ANOTHER VOICE Auberon Waugh £3.95
- ☐ ARMCHAIR GOLF Ronnie Corbett £3.50
- ☐ BEDSIDE RUGBY Bill Beaumont £3.50
- ☐ SWEETS Shona Crawford Poole £3.95
- ☐ DON'T ASK THE PRICE Marcus Sieff £3.95
- ☐ SQUASH BALLS Barry Waters £3.50
- ☐ BACK TO CAPE HORN Rosie Swale £3.95
- ☐ BY SEA AND LAND Robin Neillands £3.95

You can buy Fontana paperbacks at your local bookshop or newsagent. Or you can order them from Fontana Paperbacks, Cash Sales Department, Box 29, Douglas, Isle of Man. Please send a cheque, postal or money order (not currency) worth the purchase price plus 22p per book for postage (maximum postage required is £3).

NAME (Block letters) _____

ADDRESS _____

_____

_____

While every effort is made to keep prices low, it is sometimes necessary to increase them at short notice. Fontana Paperbacks reserve the right to show new retail prices on covers which may differ from those previously advertised in the text or elsewhere.